WARREN MILLER

BOB RIM
GLAD TO SEE
WITH YOU 'N VAIL
THANK

ON FILM IN PRINT

Written and illustrated by the same guy.

The stories in this collection were originally published in *The Vail Daily*, *The Mammoth Times*, *Ski Magazine*, *The Summit Daily*, *Snow Country*, *Impact*, *Windsurfer Magazine*, and turned down by magazines and newspapers too numerous to mention.

Published by Ritem and Printem, Inc. P.O. Box 2696, Vail, Colorado 81658.

Ritem and Printem is a Trademark of Clark, Mokey, Smith, @ Hammerschligger Ltd., Publishers to the masses.

Manufactured in the United States of America.

Library of Congress Cataloging and Publication Data.

Miller, Warren.
    Warren Miller, ON FILM, IN PRINT/ Warren Miller-1st edition. I wish I had the numbers and the information for you, but whoever is in charge of the letter "M" in the Library of Congress never returned my many phone calls or my letters. If you want further information, you can get it from the publishers, or through the ISBN number.

ISBN 0-9636144-1-X
First Edition–1994
Second Edition–1995

Dedication

Every book has one. So I guess this one should.

I was lucky enough to start at the top and have been going downhill ever since, so I would like to dedicate this book to several people. Not necessarily in alphabetical order or in the order they changed my life but significant people never the less.

Pappy Rogers let me sleep free in his Sun Valley parking lot for two long cold winters. Otto Lang gave me a job teaching kick turns at the bottom of Dollar Mountain. My two ski pupils, Hal Geneen and Chuck Percy, loaned me a 16mm camera .

When I tried to borrow $400 dollars to start my film business no one would loan me that much money, so four men loaned me $100 each. John Levy, El Jorden, Jack Given, and George Gore.

John Elvrum loaned me $67 dollars to buy six rolls of film in January 1952 to film his one chair lift at Snow Valley, California.

My three children, Scott, Chris, and Kurt for giving me reason to be me.

My wife Laurie who has to listen to me narrate our daily life the same way I narrate my movies, and is the best laundress and support system a man could ever marry.

Finally, I would like to dedicate this book to the thousands of people who have come to see my films for the last forty five years and usually left the theatre with their lives messed up.

CONTENTS

INTRODUCTION

A book usually has an introduction by some very famous person (to help sell the book) that says the author is one of several things: weird, brilliant, adventuresome, taller than you think, older than you can imagine, and/or lives a perfect life with a beautiful wife and successful children.

Since all of the famous people I approached to write an introduction to my book never returned my phone calls, I had to write it myself.

Everyone wants to travel and see the world from their first-class seat in a 500 mph airplane, ski in waist-deep powder snow from a helicopter, ride in a deluxe compartment aboard the Orient Express across Europe, ride in the only seat in a rickshaw, or hear the operatic tones of a gondolier in Venice. Never having grown up or having had a real job, I've, therefore, been there, done that, and have the T-shirt somewhere in the garage or rag bag to prove it.

When I was looking for my mountain bike and matching T-shirt the other day, I had to climb over a pile of old skis, three windsurfers, a couple of old catamaran sails, a 1968 one-of-a-kind, Hobie surfboard, four fishing poles, an old wet suit, a lawn mower with a bad intake manifold, and a snowplow that I broke when I tried to blow half a skid chain out of my driveway last February.

I have used all of this junk, as my wife refers to it, in the process of researching and producing over 500 sports movies since my first ski film at Squaw Valley, California, during the winter of 1949-50, the year they opened with only one chairlift, two rope tows, and four instructors. (On a good day, we would all have a pupil.) Several years ago, I sold my film company to my youngest son, Kurt, so now all I have to do to help create the annual Warren Miller feature ski film is to write the script and narrate it.

As a result, I had a lot of spare time on my hands, so I went out and landed my first real weekly job since I quit working as a carpenter in 1953. I managed to get a job writing a weekly column for the *Vail Daily*, a newspaper that has to tread a very fine editorial line between the guests who routinely pay $425 a day for a private ski instructor so they don't have to stand in a three minute quad lift line, and the person who loads them onto it, who are earning survival wages while living cheek-to-jowl with 11 other people in a two bedroom, one bath, 28-year-old condominium, one that is in the right neighborhood for local urban renewal politicians to bring in the bulldozers and start over.

The editor/publisher, who has since sold out and gone on to ride his mountain bike somewhere else, decided that I had a few experiences that his customers might like to read about. Since then, I have managed to save that $25 a week the newspaper has been paying me, for the occasional hamburger, fries, and chocolate shake. I have also bought a new exhaust manifold for my lawn mower that I will get around to installing, if the fishing ever slows down. Last spring, I even managed to save up five weeks' pay and took my wife out to dinner.

That $25 a week in wages used to be two weeks pay during the summer of 1942, when I was in college, and three months pay when I was delivering newspapers in 1939. But so what? Coca Cola was a nickel a bottle, gasoline cost 11 cents a gallon, you could buy a good used car for $25, and my first feature length ski film in 1950 cost $427.

Writing scripts for the hundreds of movies I produced was very simple compared to describing things *without* the aid of the following: brilliant colored images supplied by a handful of dedicated motion picture cameramen, great editors, music by contemporary musicians, meticulous post-production people, and marketers to sell the finished product. To me, the most important people in the whole equation have been those people who have been standing in line at the box office to buy tickets to the last 45 years of my films.

Recently, when the newspaper published the eulogy I read at Frank Wells' memorial service, an old friend of mine called and said,

"Warren, why don't you put all of your columns together in a book and sell them?"

Sounded like a simple idea to me.

The only difficulty I saw would be to rewrite every one of the columns for people who might never have tried skiing, boating, windsurfing, or any of the other disasters that I am constantly lurching away from, in the middle of, or just heading towards.

I tried to get a publisher to handle the whole deal for me, but I collected enough rejection slips to wallpaper my office. I also had receipts for dozens of unsuccessful attempts to talk to agents on the phone; every time I tried, I would get some sort of recorded voice mail message.

"Hello, this is Barry Mascowitz and I am either on the other phone, on a business trip looking for new writers. Submit your manuscript to my office for my consideration. Write me a letter and, in 25 words or less, tell me why I should consider your work."

I located an editor who can clean them up and punctuate them properly for me, as much as I'd let her, (Thanks, Barbara Dillman), drew the cartoons to illustrate some of the stories, located a printer (Thanks, Bob Valentine), and found an empty garage to store the books in until I could figure out how to sell all of them.

I did all of the above on an island that is a 20 minute drive to a one hour wait in line, for an hour and fifteen minute ferry boat ride to a small town on the mainland, which is then a two hour drive to a major city.

I've been making sports films for 45 years, and now I am looking forward to writing stories for the *Vail Daily*, *The Mammoth Times*, and a whole bunch of other newspapers for the next 45 years.

But I have to tell you that in today's economy, $25 a week doesn't go very far.

So, buy an extra copy of *ON FILM, IN PRINT* for a friend so they, too, can study my medical treatise, *How to Get in Shape for Skiing*, and then I can trade my reel job for a real job!

WARREN MILLER, STATISTICALLY SPEAKING

Six foot something or other, mostly bald, and weighing 205 pounds, Warren Miller is probably the world's most successful person at, "THE PURSUIT OF THE FREE LIFT TICKET."

Born in Hollywood, California, he grew up during the depression. While he was in grade school in 1936, the lure of the silver screen was prompted by his successful sale of nitrate motion picture film. Highly inflammable, these 35mm filmstrips were rolled by Warren into one inch diameter rolls and sold under the label of "STINK BOMB." When the wind was blowing in the right direction, one stink bomb would burn very slowly and produce dense smoke long enough to completely empty a schoolroom.

All of this chaos could be created for only five cents! This was Warren's first entrepreneurial venture. It was also his first travel adventure. He was transported to the superintendent of schools in a black police car.

It was very expensive to ski in those days; Warren skied for the first time on a Boy Scout trip to the nearby San Bernardino mountains in 1938. An hour long climb up the hill cost just the energy of a peanut butter sandwich and two fig bars.

Warren's first real ski adventure was ten years later on a six month trip through the ski resorts of the west. During the winter of

1946-47, accompanied by Ward Baker, they lived in the finest ski resort parking lots of the West. This included almost 100 days at Sun Valley, Idaho, in their trailer parked in the corner by the trees against the snow bank. That teardrop trailer was only eight feet long by four feet wide. Warren and Ward survived on frozen rabbits, oatmeal, oyster crackers, and ketchup. The six month long ski trip cost about eighteen cents a day.

Using an 8mm movie camera, Warren and Ward filmed each other so they could learn how to ski. This was the first of almost 500 different movies that Warren has produced so far during his 45 year career. During this time, he was also perfecting the art of almost 100 different ways to sneak onto a chairlift without paying.

The early years of motion picture production were not easy. Like the STINK BOMBS, some of his early ski films were known to empty out entire auditoriums.

Those early days of film production were tough because lift tickets cost a whopping $4 a day. However, you could buy a mountaintop hamburger for $1.25. One day, someone Warren was filming told him to join the Ski Writer's Association. The rest is history. He was put on a mailing list and, within 30 days, received 47 different season lift passes to 47 different ski resorts. Not bad for a $25 initiation fee.

After riding surfboards and racing sailboats near his film production office in Hermosa Beach, California, for 40 years, Warren has recently traded his house near the surf for a house near a gondola in Colorado. Now, instead of shoveling sand off his front yard at the beach, he shovels snow out of his driveway in the mountains.

But, the call of the surf is still strong. When the ski lifts close in the spring, word processor, printer, fax, and xerox machines re packed up and shipped to his second home on Maui. There, his windsurfer, word processor, and Don Quixote-type humor rages on, uncensored by the dictates of anyone in any business.

Somewhat mellowed by his wife, Laurie, it still remains to be seen how much of his writing will ever get published, because the stories usually hit too close to home. However, Warren's 45 years of producing, writing, and narrating the over 500 movies has pleased the people who bought the tickets to see them in a theater or those who rent the videos. Unfortunately, people in control of the industry and the insurance companies still don't like him to show people falling off chairlifts, jumping off cliffs, or crashing in sailboats.

Warren has been skiing, surfing, sailing, windsurfing, fishing, filming, drawing, and writing since the invention of most of the major ski resorts in the world. With luck, he will be around, skiing, surfing, sailing, windsurfing, fishing, filming, drawing, and writing with his off-beat humor for another 45 years at least. There are a lot more mountains to be skied, waves to be ridden, boats to be sunk, and bubbles to be burst.

Warren will probably continue to ski them, sail them, sink them, and, for darn sure, puncture them.

THE HOUSE

The other day, I was nailing shingles on the side of my new studio that I am building, when I thought about the first house I ever tried to build.

It was in Sun Valley, Idaho, during the spring of 1949.

It had been a good winter of teaching skiing and discovering a financial bonanza when I spent every spare moment dying pieces of army surplus nylon parachute cord and making shoelaces out of them.

The shoelaces are another story altogether.

I had made enough money to finally buy my first piece of real estate, a beautiful lot with Trail Creek on two sides of it, and the highway into Ketchum on the third.

I would be able to catch trout from what would eventually be my bedroom window, and I even saw a family of ducks swimming in a back eddy of the river the day I decided to buy it.

A piece of land this nice didn't come cheap, so I had to spend a lot of time negotiating with the owner. He was a good friend and former mountain guide who would guarantee you a shot at a bighorn sheep for $25. That included the horse to get you there, food, tents, and two pack animals.

We finally settled on an unheard of high price for a parcel like this, and so I wrote the biggest check of my young life.

$350!

As the snow began to melt on my property, I knew that the ski lifts would be closing soon and I knew I would have a couple of major problems in building my house.

I had gotten used to the good life of three free meals a day as a Sun Valley ski instructor. My $5 a month garage where I was painting signs and wrapping and shipping my nylon shoelaces all over America was no place for a former ski instructor to live.

I needed a night job so I could build my house during the day, a job that required no thought and yet supplied room and board. I soon became such a good dishwashing machine operator in The Challenger Inn dining room that, when they would have convention dinners over in the Lodge, I would get transferred over there.

I could handle more dishes quicker than anyone else, and stay ahead of 275 soup bowls, seafood cocktail glasses, cups, saucers, salad plates, dinner, and dessert dishes that came back to the kitchen, with or without food or cigarette butts on them.

I was earning a bed in the ski patrol barracks, three meals a day, and $100 a month. What more could a man ask for?

Now, I could begin gathering the materials to build my dream house. I borrowed a friend's pickup truck and made a lot of trips to the Triumph Mine to load crushed rock on the back of the truck, one shovelful at a time. When I got it safely to my property I would empty it a shovelful at a time. When I purchased the lumber necessary to build the forms for the foundation, the lumberyard loader told me about a cement mixer that I could probably borrow for a day or so.

I now had my own shovel, a pile of sand and gravel, a bucket to haul water from the creek, enough bags of concrete, the forms built, and I was ready to start pouring concrete. I had to wait, however, until I had the night off from washing dishes. That way, if it took longer to mix and pour the concrete than I anticipated, I wouldn't lose my great dishwashing job when I didn't show up.

My house was going to be a small one, about 800 square feet. But, when you are filling the mixer up a shovelful at a time, it takes almost 16 hours of nonstop work to shovel sand and gravel, haul water, mix cement, haul it to the form in a bucket, and repeat the process. .

I did this over and over and over, until the last few buckets full of cement were poured by the light of the occasional car that drove by my property.

Way out, by what today is the base of the Warm Springs ski lift, there was a sawmill that was powered by a sometimes running, gigantic steam engine from an old thrashing machine. Here, round logs were squared on three sides so you could stack them up into a house a lot quicker and much more easily. The price for the logs was low, the mill was only a couple of miles away, and I could get them as I needed them. When you are laying up log walls by yourself (called parbuckling), you don't want big stacks of logs laying around the property to fall over.

I was progressing rapidly on the walls during the day and washing dishes at night, when a box arrived at the Post Office.

In it was a note from two of my former ski school pupils, Hal Geneen and Chuck Percy. Chuck was the president of The Bell and Howell Camera Company and Hal Geneen was the comptroller.

In the box was a Bell and Howell 16mm model 70DA motion picture camera with three lenses, a leather carrying case, a roll of color film, and a set of directions for its use.

The note recapped the dinner we'd had together in March and apologized for not sending the camera to me sooner. They wished me well in The Travel Film Lecture business and also said that I could pay them the $216 out of my earnings when, and if, I ever made a Travel Film.

I had, by this time in the spring of 1949, already made several 8mm surfing films and had an 8mm color film record of my years of living in the parking lot at Sun Valley. If I was going to make Adventure Travel Films, there was no sense in building a house by a river in Sun Valley. I would have to travel all over the world to make my movies, so I should be living down in Hollywood where all of the film business is.

While I sat staring at this fantastic hand-wind camera, I painted a FOR SALE sign on a log on my partially built house on the river. Before I knew it, I had a buyer for the land and building. I sold everything for $900 and made $100 on the deal, not counting my labor. I packed up all of my belongings in my teardrop trailer and headed for southern California.

Three days later, I had a job testing air mattresses in an air mattress factory and started building my first waterproof camera box.

I wanted to film men riding 100 pound redwood surfboards on waves that sometimes came clear up over their shoulders.

That was 45 years and about 500 movies ago.

But now, I better get back to finishing this shingling so my studio garage will be finished, and I will have a place to store 50 years of memorabilia that I have collected while I produced those 500 sports films.

Memorabilia including, but not limited to, one high mileage, 16mm Bell and Howell hand-wind motion picture camera.

"Fashion item: In an effort to get more ski racing
on television, American designer Whinny, has
created a brand-new-for-the-nineties, ski racing
uniform for the U.S. Ski Team. A flesh colored full
body suit, with a sprayed on bikini."

FROM NOTES I TOOK AT THE OLYMPICS

When I travel, I take notes that are always difficult to figure out when I finally get back to my word processor at some uncertain time in the distant future. This is due in part to erratic bus drivers, or me driving with one hand on the steering wheel in order to take notes, on a bumpy, icy road, or being stuck in an airline seat that was designed for a four year old.

I went on a press familiarization trip to the site of the Olympics where everyone was very nice so I would be sure to come away with a good impression. As a result, my notes are a lot clearer than they usually are.

For example:

TRNSPTATION means,

"What time does the bus leave?"

"A few minutes after it gets here."

"When will it get here?"

"I don't know."

"Where did it go?"

"To one of the ski lifts."

"A T bar?"

"I don't know."

"Will it take us to the chair lift?"

"If you ask him to."

FD DRNK

"We would like a couple of cups of tea and two pastries."

"I'm sorry, but I can't sell you any because we close in half an hour."

"Where could we buy some?"

"I don't know. It is Saturday and all of the stores in town have to close at 2:00 p.m."

"Why?"

"It's the custom."

"This is a rehearsal for the Olympics next winter and I thought they would be rehearsing everything."

"We are."

"But there were over 8,000 cross-country racers in the Birkebinner this morning, and you are still closing up every store in Lillehammer today at 2:00?"

"It's the custom."

ICEHKY

"This gigantic cave was a bomb shelter during World War II. In 1950, it was made larger and converted into an underground swimming pool. Then, they had to hollow out more of the mountain for a parking lot for the swimmers. When Norway won the Olympic bid, the Government decided to make the swimming pool into an ice hockey arena that seats over 5,000 people with adequate underground parking to go with it."

"Why?"

W DH ICY

The women's downhill was boycotted by the racers during the Olympic trials because they felt it wasn't fast enough or dangerous enough.

I must be a skier from another planet than the Olympic women racers. I skied the women's downhill course the next day, and it was a two mile sideslip on ice that was so fast and so rough and chattery that it made both my socks and my long johns fall down.

MDLS

An award is being created for the ski racer who can take his ski off the fastest after going through the finish line and hold it up for the television cameras.

An instant replay of the ski removal medal winner revealing his secrets in super slow motion could be diagramed by Mr. Ace Hardware on a chalkboard diagram. It could show toe thrust, heel kick, wrist motion, and, most important, an elapsed time and motion study of down and up waist bend during ski removal because it takes the most time.

For the booking agent of the ski removal winners, this finish area television exposure is just as important as their joint bank account.

BUSERLY

The bus to watch the downhill left early so we had to grab some cold groceries and beverages from the dining room smorgasbord to eat and drink during the winding 30 mile ride. I made sure I had plenty of orange juice to spill on my wife. I also grabbed a six-pack of Norwegian flat bread. Six slices is about the size of a deck of cards, and about as tasty. In another pocket, in a baggy, I had eleven ounces of caviar pate', enough sardines for two weeks, and an extra gallon of scalding hot coffee. The extra coffee I would use later to jump start my hands by pouring hot coffee on them when they got too cold while making such hard to understand notes.

ANNCR

Ski racers leave the start every 100 seconds and the announcer describes their every move during the two minute downhill. First in Norwegian, then Swedish, German, French, Italian, and finally Russian. By the time he got around to English, the racer had already finished and was trying to win the award for the fastest ski removal in the finish area (see MDLS).

LFTS

A resort surplus T-Bar salesman must have retired on the sales he made in Norway. At one resort, they had seven of them and one short antique single chairlift. The chairlift had a long line but the T Bars were just long. The one that finally got you to the top of the hill was a mile and a half long and on a very steep sidehill. It was cleverly designed so that the two people riding it would lean away from each other and six out of seven pairs of people who started together would arrive at the top with only one person left riding.

TKTS

The lift tickets are the new, electronic kind. You slide yours into a slot and the turnstile clicks and lets you through to ride the lift. Each time you use your ticket, microscopic electronic gizmos are somehow subtracted from your innocent looking card (one electronic gizmo equals one lift ride).

You wear this ticket on an elastic string around your neck and it takes about ten rides to figure out the coefficient of elasticity of the string around your neck and how far you have to bend over each time to insert your card into the slot.

You can tell who the first time electronic ticket users are because we all have a red welt across our neck where the elastic string snaps back when you let go of the card after inserting it. It always catches you in the Adam's apple.

BNDAID

A plastic device that I began to wear over my Adam's apple while I skied at the many different locations where the Olympic races will be held in Lillehammer.

So much for clear notes and bandaids.

MONKEYING AROUND ON SKIS

In the late 1930's, any hill with a rope tow was called a ski resort. Never mind that it had a small, always muddy or frozen, parking lot and that the rope tow always broke while you were hanging onto it in the middle of the afternoon.

If a rope tow was a ski resort, then there used to be a ski resort where Universal Studios stands today in North Hollywood.

On a fairly flat hill with a view of the San Fernando Valley and all of the orange trees, Austrian ski instructor, Sepp Benedicter, hung the upper sheave of a rope tow from an oak tree; the power to run the rope came from the jacked-up back wheel of his Model A Ford.

In place of snow, he and some of his friends had hauled a couple of truckloads of pine needles down from the San Bernardino mountains and spread it around with pitchforks and rakes.

This was probably the first time I ever witnessed anyone making a turn on a pair of skis, as Sepp instructed three or four people in the intricacies of the snowplow turn.

I had ridden my blue balloon-tired bicycle from downtown Hollywood up over Cahuenga Pass into the San Fernando Valley. I did it because of a new tourist attraction that I had read about. The admission was ten cents and it was built right near the first valley stop on The Pacific Electric Railroad, the route of The Big Red Cars.

Monkey Island!

Some investor had built a 40 foot high, fake plaster and cement mountain and surrounded it with a 20 foot wide moat of slimy green, stagnant water. You paid your ten cents and then got to stand and watch about 100 undernourished monkeys sitting on the concrete mountain sullenly watching you watching them.

For another five cents, you could buy a big bag of peanuts to throw at the monkeys. If the peanuts fell in the water, the more adventuresome monkeys would wade out and pick them up one by one. Some paying customers tested them to see if they would wade out into the deeper water. They wouldn't, or so I thought.

I was told later by the combination ticket seller, ticket taker, peanut salesman, monkey keeper, owner, that the monkeys had been disappearing one by one. He had finally figured out that they were learning to swim across the moat at night and escape the concrete island.

His suspicions had been confirmed just the day before when an alert newspaper photographer had snapped a picture of a monkey in an orange tree about half a mile away.

As I gazed across Monkey Island and tried unsuccessfully to understand all of the potential ramifications of such a money making tourist attraction, I could see some movement on the hill that was about half a mile away. It looked as though half a dozen bent-over people were sliding up and down the ridge below the solitary oak tree.

Since I had now gotten tired of the morose monkeys staring at me staring at them, I climbed on my blue bicycle and pedaled over to see what was going on at the lone oak tree on the green grass meadow.

There, I saw a genuine 1937 rope tow and some skiers having a grand old time. It was so hot that several of the skiers were making their turns without shirts.

I laid my bicycle down and walked up in the tall, green grass to watch them make turns on pine needles and squashed green grass that was already turning various shades of yellow and brown.

For the first time in my life, I heard words spoken in German, words like stembogen, vorlage, and sitzmark, to mention just a few, words that you never hear on a ski hill anymore.

The ski slope could not have been longer than a couple of hundred feet and I was awestruck when I got to the top of the slope and sat down under the oak tree.

The people on skis were free to go wherever their skis wanted to take them. I was really excited about being a spectator to such an unbelievable sight. The only spectator, I might add. About the time I was absorbing all of these new sights for a 12 year old, the remains of an acorn landed right in front of me. Then another and another.

Looking up, I saw three of the escapees from Monkey Island. They had found an ample supply of acorns to live on and enough crazy skiers to watch to keep them completely amused. Not only had they learned to swim, they had learned to throw nuts back at people.

The next weekend, I brought a friend of mine on the bicycle trip over Cahuenga Pass to see Monkey Island and The Oak Tree Ski Resort.

There was a closed sign on the entrance to the tourist attraction, the water had been drained out of the moat, the monkeys were all gone, and so was the rope tow.

Sepp Benedicter, with his rope tow and his band of beginning skiers, had moved down to a sand dune near 34th Street in Manhattan Beach for the summer.

I learned at a very young age, that if that stuff that you slide on that is supposed to be under your skis isn't there, and the lift to get you back to the top of the hill is gone, don't monkey around; go to where they are!

"Anyone on skis, was free to go wherever their skis would take them ."

THE SECOND SKI TRIP

I sat on the curb waiting for my ride to pick me up. Each time I exhaled, my breath was a misty cloud that was backlit by the glare of the one bright street light half a block away. It was already after 4:00 A.M. and I wondered why my ride hadn't shown up yet. Overhead, a million or so stars were shimmering on this very cold January morning in 1938, very cold for southern California. It was probably down into the low forties. Maybe even down into the 30's, I hoped.

My pine skis and bamboo poles were lying in the wet grass alongside my canvas rucksack. In my rucksack were four peanut butter and jam sandwiches, four fig bars, and an apple.

I was wearing my nearly new Sears and Roebuck fake Levi's that cost one dollar instead of the two that real Levi's cost. I wore a pair of almost knee-high hiking boots that had a small pocket on the outside of the right boot that held my pocketknife. I never hiked without a knife in it, in case I got bitten by a rattlesnake. I didn't yet know what I would do if I did get bitten, but I sure had the right kind of knife, just in case. My wool socks, with the red stripes around the top, were turned down over the top of the boots, and I had a wool shirt on over my sweatshirt.

This was my second trip to the snow. Learning from the bitter cold experience of my first trip, I had visited the one Army Surplus store left in Los Angeles, down on Main Street.

The surplus was all over 20 years old and left over from World War I. I had spent almost all day deciding on what I just couldn't do without, and had finally parted with 25 cents of my hard earned money for a black wool hat. Even in 1940, War Surplus stores were on Main Street and had creaky oak floors and barrels of all kinds of stuff you just couldn't do without. I had also paid ten cents for a pair of cotton gloves that I had soaked in melted paraffin to make them really waterproof.

Born and raised in southern California, I had no cold weather experience and had never even heard of long underwear, much less seen a pair of them. However, on my first trip to the snow, I had frozen my buns, so I was, I thought, wisely wearing my cotton pajamas under my Sears and Roebuck Levi's.

My adrenalin was really keeping me warm in anticipation of my first genuine Boy Scout ski trip to Mt. San Jacinto, high above Palm Springs.

As the cold began to creep into my skinny, teenage body and overcome the adrenalin, a pair of headlights turned the corner and headed down my dark street.

I was the last one to be picked up, joining David, Bill, Jim, George, and John. John was the rich one in the group and had his own four-door sedan. Our obligation was to each kick in thirty cents for our share of the gas for the long, three hour trip. The big black 1935 Chevrolet had big wide running boards, straight sides, a flat roof, and windows that rolled up and down. It also had a spare tire mounted on the back. We stuffed our three pair of skis and poles between the tire and the back of the car and tied them there.

Ski racks had not yet been invented.

Only three of us had skis and poles. David, Bill, and George had come along for the ride and the hike up to the snow. I didn't know it then, but they were planning on taking turns with my pine skis and bamboo poles when I got too tired to climb up and try to ski down.

Two hours later, we were leaving the small, flat town of Hemet and beginning the long climb up the winding road to the trail head. Part way up Mt. San Jacinto, the stars began to fade and the clear black sky began to turn grey in the east. Across the valley to the east, 10,000 foot high Mt. San Gorgonio was taking shape and was covered halfway down in a deep blanket of snow.

We finally ground to a stop at the end of the narrow, winding road, climbed out, stiff and sore from the long cramped ride, and began to unload the car. Just as people have been doing since the first person ever went on a ski trip in an automobile and still do today, the first thing we did was unload the skis and lean them against the side of the car. As soon as we got all three pairs of skis lined up nicely, they fell over and scratched the right front fender.

The same thing still happens, almost sixty years later.

Sitting on the running board for a few minutes while everyone got their stuff together and organized their packs, I managed to scarf down two of my four peanut butter sandwiches, as well as half of my fig bars. (Even today, I still eat fig bars at exciting times in my life!) I was going on the theory that my pack would be better balanced if half of the weight was in my stomach and half of it was in my rucksack.

Finishing that, I put my rucksack over my bony shoulders and then, with my skis over my right shoulder just as I had seen in the poster at the sporting good store, we began the long climb up to where we hoped there would be some snow left from the last storm.

Johnny immediately started singing, and we all joined in a robust, yet slightly altered, version of "When Johnny Comes Marching Home Again, Hurrah, Hurrah!"

The Boy Scout chorale lasted for about the first 200 yards; then we gave that up and settled for just gasping for breath instead. Our bodies were set for sea level and we were at almost 9,000 feet.

The decomposed granite that this ancient mountain was made of crunched under our feet, and the screech of the Blue Jay replaced the screech of the sea gull that we were all used to. This seemed to me to be the real essence of what belonging to the Boy Scouts was all about: exploration, discovery, adventure, being out of breath, and sweating a lot because of all of the clothes I had covered my body with.

About four or five miles up the trail, we finally reached the first patch of snow. At this point, we were again led by our brilliant patrol leader and crossed over and continued to climb on the sunny south-facing side of the canyon where what snow there had been had already melted. After about three hours of climbing, resting, and climbing, we found a patch of snow that was big enough and deep enough to handle five or six turns. We also chose that one because Johnny showed us how we could walk up on the dirt beside the snow patch in our boots and carry our skis.

The patch of snow was about 30 feet wide, 100 feet long, and about six inches deep. It was the biggest patch we could find that was still left over from a three weeks ago storm, hard and crusty from constant melting and freezing.

Today, we would call it corn snow.

John had a pair of genuine ridge top skis with metal edges, metal Kandahar bindings, real ski boots with box toes, and varnished split bamboo ski poles. He even had a ski hat and most important, a very rich father.

He also had a copy of Otto Lang's, *Downhill Skiing* book that he pulled out of his rucksack. Before we put on our skis, we sat on a rock at the top of this virgin snow-field and turned the pages until we got beyond the walking in the flat and the kick turn chapters to get to the real good stuff; it was time to try to learn the snowplow turn.

Traversing in the melting snow had gotten progressively easier on my skis without edges and toe strap bindings. About the tenth time, I began to get close to the edge of the snow-field and start dragging my poles more and more aggressively. I managed to occasionally come to a stop before I slid out onto the gravel where I would stop in only about one ski length.

There, I would pick myself up from the dirt and step out of my two dollar pine skis with the toe straps, bend over, pick them up and point them back in the other direction, and begin to try to traverse back. Before I could move, though, I had to slide them back and forth to get the mud off the bottom of them.

Johnny was really hot. He had already mastered the snowplow turn when his dad took the whole family to Yosemite for the Christmas holidays. He had actually stayed in a hotel and eaten in restaurants and ridden on a ski lift. He had been taught how to ski at Badger Pass, from Hannes Schroll and Sigi Engle.

It was a real thrill for me to watch him make linked snowplow turns down the face of that flat snowfield in the meadow where the snow had blown in. After watching him for four or five runs, I knew it was time for me to not just traverse, but to try to turn my pine skis with the leather toe straps. As I attempted to turn the first time, absolutely nothing happened. My heels went apart and my toes were pointing at each other, but my skis were still going straight, in what, even today, could still be called a parallel traverse.

While I climbed up beside the snowfield to try my next traverse, I figured out the following: if I tried to curl up my toes in my soft leather boots, this might tighten up the toe straps and, at the same time, put a little more pressure on my heels. This didn't work any better than the previous attempts, as I once again kept accelerating and slid out onto the gravel where I fell to a stop.

This time as I was climbing back up, I took out my pocketknife (that was reserved for cleaning out rattlesnake bites) from the pocket on my right boot, and cut a few branches from a small tree. At the top, after I climbed into my skis, I jammed these twigs under the toes of my flexible boots.

This should tighten up my toe straps and give me some more control over my skis. I picked up one foot, wiggled it, and the ski that was attached actually moved in synchronization with the foot.

Sort of.

Realistically, there was still about ten or fifteen degrees of slop at each end of the wiggle.

"O.K this is it." I bent over into the already famous Otto Lang crouch, and started across in my usual parallel ski traverse.

"Now go into a snowplow and shift the weight to the downhill ski."

Right?

Wrong!

I traversed about five or six ski lengths and had already accelerated to about 103 m.p.h. when I went into my first ever snowplow position. My binding-tightening twigs had already vibrated out from under my right hiking boot, so that foot went into the snowplow position, just as I had directed it to.

But the ski didn't.

The twigs under my left boot apparently had been wedged in tighter than the right foot so, as I shoved that ski out into the snowplow position, it did as it was supposed to do. As it almost reached the correct angle of the snowplow position, I heard the splintering of wood and the toe strap pulled the top of the left ski right off.

Not very good pine.

The heel of my right boot was now dragging in the snow outside of that ski, and attached to my left foot was a toe strap, a bunch of twigs, and a piece of a pine ski about fifteen inches long.

Skiing was over for me.

On this trip anyway.

The rest of us sat and watched Johnny herringbone up and snowplow down for another hour and a half as we scarfed the balance of our lunches, sucked on melted snow, and began to talk about the long hike back down to the car.

The sun was warm enough to take off our shirts and soak it up as we finished our lunches. Overhead, the blue jays instinctively sat in the branches and screeched, waiting for us to leave so they could pick up whatever crumbs we might have dropped.

Johnny finally got tired and quit, so we all got our gear together and headed back down to the car. I carried the remains of one of my two dollar skis in my rucksack and the other ski over my shoulder. I knew I could glue the parts back together in my wood shop class at Thomas Starr King Junior High School.

When we got to the car, we were greeted by a flat tire and a spare with no air in it.

It didn't take too long to jack the car up and, with tire irons, get the tire off the rim, pump up the tube, and then draw straws to see who would have to hike down to the nearby creek and sink the tube in a pond to try to locate the leak by looking for escaping bubbles.

Bill lost, and while he was doing that, we tied the skis on the back of the car and loaded the rucksacks in the running board rack. When Bill returned with the leaking inner tube, it didn't take too long to sandpaper around the hole, apply the glue to the tube and the patch, and then clamp them together for a few minutes. Now the tube was reinserted in the tire, man-handled onto the rim with the tire irons, and pumped up until it was hard enough to drive on.

It was already dark as we finally got underway; we could see the lights of Hemet far below and San Bernardino off in the distance, as Johnny wheeled the black Chevrolet down the winding mountain road.

Before we had driven three miles, I was sound asleep. How long I slept I don't know, but I woke up to the squeal of tires with the car leaning precariously to the right in a tight left turn, and then we were upside down and flying, crashing, bouncing, and rolling amidst the grinding of metal and the crashing of glass. I knew we were all in trouble.

When the noise and the frightening motion of the wreck settled down, I crawled around in broken glass on the roof of the car, wiggled out through the broken window next to where I had been sitting, and fell in a heap in a ditch alongside the upside down car.

Everyone was shouting back and forth.

"Are you O.K.?"

"Yeah!"

"I think I'm O.K.!"

Everyone answered O.K. except me.

It was obvious to me that my arm was badly broken and my wrist was dislocated. My Boy Scout training took over and I wouldn't let anyone move me until medical help arrived.

It seemed like forever before they did. I lay there in the darkness, looking up at the same zillions of stars I had been looking at early the same morning.

The help that arrived was the local veterinarian on his was home from delivering a couple of lambs at a nearby farm. It only took him a couple of minutes to figure out the extent of my injuries.

He said, simply,

"No problem."

"One of you hold his upper arm; I'll just pull his hand out a little and the dislocated wrist will kick back into place. The broken bone should be fine. I'll squeeze it back into the position it belongs in and splint it. When you get him back home, he can get an x-ray if he wants to. There shouldn't be any problem."

When that veterinarian pulled on my hand to straighten out my broken arm and dislocated wrist, it seemed like he had stretched it out to where it was about eleven feet long. When he finally let go of it, I passed out from the pain. (Later in life, I learned I didn't have a "threshold of pain"...there just wasn't one. I don't like it and I don't want any, anymore!)

Next thing I knew, everyone had somehow turned the car right side up and figured that it was in good enough shape to still drive it back to Los Angeles.

I climbed into the back seat and tried to get comfortable while the shock of the accident kept the pain from bothering me too much, I even managed to doze off a few times.

All I could think of at that moment was,

"I wonder if my arm will be well before all of the snow melts."

We arrived back at my house just before midnight. It was completely dark. Everyone had to be sound asleep, but I knew where a key was hidden. In my shocked condition, I thought I could sneak upstairs and into bed without waking anyone up.

No such luck.

As soon as I got up on the front porch, I dropped my skis because I was trying to carry them with one hand. Lights instantly went on all over the house.

The front door opened before I could dig the key out of its hiding place, and there my mother stood.

I kind of tried to smile as she saw my sling and pale face. As I started through the front door, the narrow escape in the accident and everything else sort of got to me. I managed a perfect, projectile vomit all over her and the living room rug.

"My almost, knee length hiking boots had a pocket for my knife, in case of snake bites."

A WARM WINTER DAY

It was an unusually warm day for December. Knee high waves were crisply breaking across the reef at Malibu, and I was the only person there surfing them. It was my third year of surfing in a long-ago, time frame. A time when, if the second carload of surfers showed up, I would think Malibu was crowded.

I had spent the last three hours paddling my 11 foot, 106 pound, solid redwood surfboard back out to catch yet another small wave. I was a 17-year-old, senior in high school, and I had a lot of important things on my mind that warm winter day: my morning paper route, learning how to ride my $7 surfboard, who I should try to get a date with for the senior prom, wondering where I would get the $6 for a pair of racing tights so I could race in the upcoming Herald Express Speed Skating Championships. Important things like that.

I finally decided to go stag to the senior prom and try to dance with everyone else's date, and the $8 I would spend for the corsage and dinner party for two would easily buy my much needed pair of speed skating tights. (Not too dumb.) What was left over would buy a lot of gas for another of my surfing trips. Gasoline had already gone sky high, to 11 cents a gallon.

The most important thing I had to think about, however, was wondering when the wind would come up and freeze me out of the crystal clear, glassy water. (It would be almost a decade before the wet suit came on the surfing scene.) The wind never did blow, so exhaustion finally began to set in about 1:00 pm. When it did, I dragged my tired body and surfboard out of the water and climbed up the gently sloping beach 100 feet or so. There, I sat down alongside a toasty warm sand dune where I had hidden my lunch.

Watching a trio of brown pelicans glide along the face of an approaching wave, I started munching on the first of three peanut butter and jelly sandwiches.

Half an hour later, after finishing the sandwiches and a quart of milk, I lay down against the warm side of the sand dune and soon fell sound asleep.

I awoke with a start, shivering in the long shadows of the late afternoon, winter sun. A slight wind had sprung up and was gently moving the grass in the sand dune.

Standing up rather stiffly, I stretched and brushed the sand off, then lifted my heavy, redwood surfboard onto my shoulder and began to walk back up to the point so I could ride a few more waves before driving back home in the Sunday afternoon traffic.

I surfed all alone for what was left of the afternoon and enjoyed the cold December waves that were clean, crisp, and very small. The slight winter sunburn I had made me feel great.

A half dozen waves later, I decided to call it quits. I pulled out of a wave at the end of a ride and paddled on down toward the hole in the fence. Crossing the much narrower beach, I climbed up the dirt bank and slid my board through the small hole in the wire fence that I had cut when I arrived early that morning.

I wiggled through the same small hole, and then dragged my heavy, long board up and carried it over to my old convertible Buick and slid it down through the back window.

Now, I began the ritual of showering with the gallon jug of water that I had left on the hood of the car all day to heat up. It felt great! I knew that I was one of the luckiest people in the world. I had discovered the freedom of standing up on a surfboard three summers before, in 1939. I had one day a week access to my sister's car, enough money to buy gas for it from my morning paper route, and I owned my very own redwood surfboard. What else could a teenager want?

The board sticking out of the back window of my car always looked like the world's largest tongue depressor. I climbed into the front seat and started the gas guzzling, eight cylinder engine. Glancing south, I couldn't see a single car headed north on the Coast highway. When I glanced over my left should, not a single southbound car was visible. It was as though traffic had come to a halt on this Sunday afternoon in December. It certainly looked like it would be an easy drive home with little or no traffic.

"Maybe a little Artie Shaw music or some Glen Miller," I thought, as I twirled the knob on the sometimes-it-works, car radio.

Switching it on, I was listening to Glenn Miller's, "Moonlight Serenade," when an announcer cut in,

"We interrupt this music to, once again, bring you this news bulletin."

"This morning at 8:05, The Imperial Japanese Navy launched a devastating attack on Pearl Harbor. Many ships have been sunk and casualties are reported as very high. We are standing by for further word from President Roosevelt at the White House."

What were you doing December 7, 1941, the day I was riding waves all by myself, on The Point at Malibu?

"Knee high waves were crisply breaking across the reef at Malibu."

GERIATRIC GENOCIDE

It is hot and windy as we stand here on the west end of the Island of Maui. Not counting our guide, the combined ages of the three of us total 192 years divided almost equally. So, the 11 mile channel between here and the Island of Molokai is a scary obstacle for us and our sailboards. Out in the center of the channel, the heavy wind is blowing the top two or three feet off the big Pacific swells.

Barbara Guild has spent a week organizing the trip and now she has become a little apprehensive because she is 64 years old.

Her husband, Don, has his silver brain bucket clamped down around his ears in case he launches off the top of a big Pacific swell and crashes. Don is more apprehensive because he is the youngest of the three of us, at 63 years of age. I'm the senior citizen of the group at 65, and I'm most apprehensive because the chase boat driver we hired got busted last night with the wrong stuff in his glove compartment and he and his latest spousal equivalent are sleeping it off in the slammer in Kahalui.

In my backpack, now readied for the crossing, is a life saving can of air-temperature, 82 degree Diet Coke, eight fig bars, a screw driver, a spare fin, 20 feet of duct tape, an extra universal, and a tube of underwater ding repair in case I hit a whale or a shark. I have carefully wrapped each item in Saran Wrap so they won't get wet when I fall, which I know I will.

Our guide, Alan Cadiz, has given each of us a flare in case we get separated, which I know we will. Now, with that six-inch-long "instrument of instant savior under any circumstances" tucked away in our rucksacks, we get down to arguing specifics.

What size sail shall we use?

Cadiz finally opts for a 4.5 meter sail after discussing the pros and cons of being over- powered against underpowered. He is our mentor and our Guru, so we all rig the same size sail as he does, carefully taking into consideration the size of our boards, the angle of the wind, its potential velocity change, and the chance that we might have to float around all night somewhere in the rumored-to-be, shark-infested ocean west of Molokai, if we guess wrong or forget about our weight differential, which I did.

By the time we get our sails rigged, a six-pack of flip-flop clad, alabaster-white, 51 inch waisted, aloha shirted and mumu clad couples have gathered around us. You can tell the men from the women by which one of them is smoking the cigar. You know who is with whom by their matching varicose veins, Aloha shirts, and who is directing who with the video cameras.

"Are those boards dangerous?"

"Are they hard to ride?"

"Do they cost very much?"

"Will they go very fast?"

"How long does it take to learn to ride one?"

"Why are you going there on them?"

"Let's go back to Lahaina and ride the glass bottom boat that leaves at noon."

One final check of our gear and we go in search of our respective bushes to handle our decreased bladder control due to the adrenalin rush thinking about the 11 miles of bumpy open ocean that separates the Island of Maui from the Island of Molokai. I watch Alan, our guide, step on his board and sail slowly away, looking back like a wagon train boss rounding up the strays. He is followed by Barbara, then Don, and finally I get my act together and leave the hot sand of Maui for the challenge of the crossing.

My thoughts?

The pro sailboarders race back and forth across this channel as though it was a small local lake. "NBD," as they call it. "No big deal."

Now the Walter Mitty in me begins to take over as the board is planing and it feels like it will be less than an hour before we are on the beach on Molokai, 11 miles away.

Alan has given his office instructions to call the Coast Guard helicopter if we are not back on Maui by 5:30. The first mile or two is a hoot and a half, as we are all hooked in and flying. Don's silver brain bucket is flashing across the channel as he chases his wife of 35 years.

Alan is racing ahead and then jibing down the face of over half-mast-high ground swells and sailing back to me, when suddenly the wind drops from twenty-plus to about six. I'm in the water before I can say,

"I should've used a bigger sail."

My rucksack is full of water because the drain holes I cut in them are all plugged up with the Saran Wrap that is supposed to be wrapped around my eight fig bars. With four gallons of water for ballast, a water start is impossible in the now, very light wind.

Alan insists on taking my rucksack. Later, I will remember that he is also taking my security blanket, the rescue flare, with him. Barbara is now about a mile ahead of me, closely followed by Don. I now realize that I outweigh Barbara by about 80 pounds, Alan by 60, and Don by 40, and we all have the same size sails.

Dumb.

Really Dumb.

Soon the wind is so light, no one is in their harness or their footstraps and I still have seven of the eleven miles to go. Even without the rucksack full of figbars and water, I can barely do a "hold the mast at the bottom," water start. The rest of the group only has six miles to go, so I don't have an option, except to try to catch up with them. Anyway, the wind is always supposed to come up stronger in the middle of the channel.

Fifteen minutes later it does, and I take off like a cut cat dipped in turpentine and slowly gain on the group.

It's a real rush to fly down the face of a big swell and scare up flying fish. Most of them explode from the face of the swell and glide off to leeward. Suddenly, two of them explode and sail upwind towards the top of the wave. These two fish have never had the velocity and direction of a sailboard put into the avoidance chip of their computer, so their brains miscalculate and one of them bounces off my sail just back of the mast and above the boom. The other one somehow manages to alter course at the last instant and zings between the mast and my front leg. The adrenalin rush of watching the fish is indescribable as they fold their wings and drop, scared spitless, back into their own saltwater world.

Our guide, Alan, told us before we left, "Keep your eye on the house in the canyon with the trees in it, two canyons to the south of the big rock. That's where we will try to land." About the time I can finally make out the rusting car under the tree by the house, the wind has dropped to barely steerage way. I now get to try to sail over a reef with half-mast high waves.

By the time I get to the surf line, Alan, Don, and Barbara are already through it and safely gliding over the reef towards shore.

Not enough wind to jibe so I can pick the right wave of a set. I just have to pump the sail hard at the right time and hope I have the reef figured out. My brain clicks back into the 1941 mode when I started surfing at Malibu, so catching the just right wave is not a problem. Success! I'm on a glassy wave all alone, just like Malibu in 1941. Now, all I have to do is sail a careful course through the hopefully, fin-deep water the last 200 yards to shore.

I know a wave breaks in water as deep as the wave is high, so if I see any wave break that is smaller than ten inches, I know that the water is less than ten inches deep and I will break off my fin on the reef.

"We made it."

As I drag my rig up onto the eight-foot-wide sandy beach, Alan, Barbara, and Don are rapidly scarfing down their lunch. It's already 4:00, and we have to be back in Lahaina by 5:30 or Alan's office is scheduled to call the Coast Guard.

"We have to leave right away."

And I just got here.

Error in communication. Barbara said she was going to bring the lunch. She forgot mine, so my eight fig bars and the can of 82 degree Diet Coke will be my fuel for the return trip. Since I was the slowest sailing over, I volunteered to leave first, knowing Don, Alan, and Barbara would pass me on the way back.

My 65 birthdays have already taken their toll on the way over and my body feels like it is part of an eighteen-wheeler road-kill on I-70. Adrenalin helps me sail back out through the shallow reef with all of the colorful sea life; then come the half mast-high waves with a light wind.

Piece of cake!

I luckily hit a lull in the swells just exactly right and am outside the surfline, relaxed and slowly cruising, waiting for Alan, Barbara, and Don. I'm cruising, but without enough wind to get in the straps or harness. And then, ever so slowly, as if in deference to my age and my salvation, the wind begins to fill in and I ease into the trapeze, then the straps and, before I know it, I am really hauling. I sail about a mile or so and then jibe on the face of a big swell because I can't see any other sails over my shoulder.

Later, I found out that Don had started a couple of minutes after I had and had been hammered in a big set of waves with no wind to bail him out. He washed around for almost 30 minutes. Alan and Barbara spent almost 45 minutes being pounded in the same reef break without wind before they finally made it outside.

All of this time Alan had his rucksack, Don's rucksack, and mine, without the fig bars, but each rucksack contained one of the three safety flares

Dumb.

Now I am out into the heavier wind that exactly matches my sail size and am really cooking and becoming hypnotized by the many flying fish I was scaring up. I was on exactly the right angle of sail so I could slide off the face of a big groundswell and race along for what seemed like half an hour. If you try to describe this euphoric feeling to someone, don't bother because they won't understand.

Looking back over my shoulder for the umpteenth time, I finally see a flash of silver and a speck of yellow sail on the horizon. Don and his silver brain bucket! Knowing that Don wouldn't leave his wife to die in the channel, she has to be close behind with Alan and his three rucksacks full of spare parts and all three safety flares.

Ahead of me now is a big tourist-hauling, Lahaina catamaran, roaring downwind towards home port with a boat load of "lobster red, day trippers." With a little course adjustment, I can sneak up on their starboard quarter and grandstand a little. After all, I'm a senior citizen on a sailboard, just finishing a round trip to Molokai and back.

"Why not go for it?"

I'm about 100 yards away before any of the lobster-red tourists see me closing fast. Now it is final decision time. Shall I reach off on the next wave and show off by pulling a jibe just before I get to the boat?

Shall I accelerate and sail in front of it?

Shall I take their stern and wave as I go by and then jibe later with a little more room to clear their bow as I come back on starboard?

I sail by their stern with my bald head shining in the afternoon sun. Senior citizen at the attack mode. As I start to pull off a clean jibe, my tired, old body again reminds me that it thinks it has been run over by an eighteen-wheeler.

Nothing works.

I perform a rare, "9.7, catapult, face plant, splash jibe."

So much for my senior citizen athletic excellence.

Amidst the hoots and hollers of the Kansas Catamaran passengers, I manage a water start and am once again crossing the catamaran's stern as I reach away from the Lahaina shore. I can now see Don's sail more easily and behind him are two yellow dots, Alan's and Barbara's sails. Jibing back again towards Lahaina, I relax, knowing that the three of them are not dead after all.

But will we make it in time to call off the Coast Guard?

Suddenly, right in my path looms Myrtle the turtle, basking in the late afternoon sun. There's her sister, Pearl, and her brother, Murdock. I'm in the middle of the breeding ground of the rare, three foot in diameter Hawaiian turtle. If you so much as touch one of these endangered floating rafts and get caught, it's an automatic $5,000 fine. That's expensive turtle soup. I manage to miss at least half a dozen of Myrtle's cousins. If I hit any one of them, it would rip the fin right out of the bottom of my board. Now the water is getting shallower, until I know my fin is going to hit the bottom, when, splat.

I'm in the lee of a megabuck destination hotel with absolutely zero wind, with still 100 yards or so to get to the shore and it is already after 5pm. Swimming my rig the last 100 yards to shore takes forever because I am now really worrying about Alan's office calling the Coast Guard.

Onshore, I am desperately looking for a pay phone, while running, slipping, and sliding, through the lobby of this gaudy pink, high-rise hotel. I'm beat, harness clad, and disheveled from all day in the warm, tropical water. I finally find the phone after recovering from three slides on my behind on the ivory smooth, simulated Polynesian floors.

The Hawaiian phone operator won't take my Colorado phone company credit card, so I manage to panhandle a quarter from a senior citizen lady tourist in a polyester dress and nurse's shoes. I dial the number and get Alan's answering machine that tries to sell me "Alan Cadiz class windsurfing lessons at Kanaha from noon till dark six days a week." I leave a message that they won't get till tomorrow and slip slide my way back to the beach.

The sun is now shining brightly off Don's silver brain bucket and, not too far behind, are Alan and Barbara.

Alan sails right to the beach and steps off his rig. With true professionalism, he pulls a quarter out of his trunks while running to the phone, and dials a secret number five minutes before they were supposed to call the Coast Guard.

Too tired to de-rig I lurched to the expensive convenience store and bought a six- pack of Diet Cokes and a six-pack of ice cream sandwiches. Ten minutes later, while sitting on the beach by our rigs watching the wind slowly drop as the sun sets Don said,

"You know Warren, for awhile out there I thought we were committing Geriatric Genocide."

IN PURSUIT OF ADVENTURE

"A journey in a boat is not a lineal experience on a given compass heading. Rather, it is an experience involving the outer reaches of your psyche, a trip glued together by your own strength, daring, and an urge to explore. All of which is mixed together with a very conscious fear of death by drowning."

My notes from the inner reaches of survival are dredged up from unwritten stuff lodged somewhere in my memory bank that are triggered by smells, motion, cold, rain, isolation, exploration, fears, whales, porpoises, and a sturdy 20 foot boat with a small cutty cabin to sleep in, powered by a 175 horsepower outboard motor that ran most of the time.

For $5, Cap Sante Marine in Anacortes, Washington, will launch any boat up to 20 feet. You gas it yourself and fill the water tanks. Our water tank was a six gallon Gatorade sports thermos. Taking up <u>all</u> of the space in the cockpit was a rolled up inflatable dinghy, a one-and-a-half horsepower motor for the dinghy, a crab pot, a shrimp pot, salmon fishing gear, a Coleman stove, a Coleman lantern, a chemical toilet, and two ice chests.

We also had enough clothes, cameras, food, books, charts, and spare parts for a four year trip around the world.

It had been a long trailer haul up from Marina Del Rey in southern California, the only

Marina in the world that is the home of 6,000 boats, 1,000 airline captains, and 4,000 stewardesses. It used to be the home port for my wife, Laurie, and I.

A freeway runs the 1,200 miles from Los Angeles, California, to Anacortes, Washington, so towing the boat was simply a matter of staying awake for the 22 hours of driving time. We did this by renting half a dozen books on tape and listening to them while driving through some of the most scenic country in the world.

Scenery that is pierced every ten miles or so with $50,000 signs rising 240 feet in the air on top of iron posts extolling the virtues of "our fast food is faster than their fast food."

"Discount gasoline."

"SHADY REST MOTEL. Take the next off ramp and come back three and a half miles and enjoy our waterbeds and cable TV."

How can you enjoy cable TV when you have just driven 943 miles since sunup and the sun is about to come up again?

At Cap Sante Marine in Anacortes, we unloaded the 14 boxes and bags of stuff for our three week cruise into the wilds of southern British Columbia, with intermittent stops among the San Juan Islands. Pat Dickson, himself, launched our boat while Laurie parked our van and trailer. (We lost Pat to cancer, recently, after many years of his keeping us afloat and alive, getting us out of numerous jams in our various boats.)

As I gassed up, I could look to the east and see Mt. Baker through eyes unaccustomed to the clear, blue sky of the Northwest. The mountain is at least 55 miles away but seemed less than a mile, its glaciers a mixture of wind-driven dirt and new avalanches cutting ribbons of white down its snow-covered volcanic sides.

I had produced an advertising film for Slickcraft boats and was so impressed with the way their 20 foot Pursuit was built, I bought it to use as a camera boat for all of the sailing films I was then producing. My other boating experience had been in racing catamarans, where even a few pounds makes a difference in what place you will finish in the race. Being new to powerboats, I assumed everyone took this much stuff with them when they boated. (Or maybe they don't have wives). I didn't know there were small villages and gas docks every 20 miles or so all the way to Alaska. There is even the occasional hotel that can almost guarantee same day room service.

After I signed the charge for the gas and premix, I climbed up on top of the driver's seat to start the engine because the cockpit of the boat was so full of our 14 boxes of stuff for the long trip ahead that our small boat was now standing room only.

The 175 horsepower outboard coughed, spit and sputtered, and finally roared into life. Engines always roar into life when you read about them. This one made a bigger racket than normal because I had forgotten to lower it into the water.

At this same very loud moment, I discovered I had forgotten to replace the drain plug in the bottom of the boat. I found this out because the gas dock lady kept blowing her air horn and screaming at me as she pointed out that we were settling by the stern. The outboard motor lower unit was for now, at least, in the water. It took me 31 gallons of water-flooding-in-time to crawl over the additional 43 bags and boxes of essentials Laurie had picked up at Safeway for our trip. I yanked up the rear floorboards, reached down in the ice cold water, and screwed the plug back in to stop the flooding of oily saltwater. I could then hear the hum of the bilge pump when the gurgle of the water going out the side of the boat exceeded what was coming into the bottom of it.

Ten minutes later, Laurie cast off as I somehow found reverse on the engine controls and made my first powerboat discovery. They pivot around their props, not around the keel like the sailboats I had been racing for the last 20 years.

The brand new captain of a brand new 38 foot Bayliner flying bridge model also found out where boats pivot when I backed into his port side at four knots. Luck was on his side, however, because the hole I put in his boat was above the water line. I would find out later he had at least ten minutes more powerboat driving experience than I had.

"Take it out of reverse, you Klutz!"

I did, but I jammed it into fast forward. The boat jumped forward 50 feet, rammed into the dock, and stopped instantly. My wife, with the bowline still in her hand, kept right on going across the deck of our boat and the gas dock, and then did a spectacular one-and-a-half into the ice cold, oily water on the far side, splashing down between the dock and the bow of a salmon trawler that was refueling on the other side.

Fortunately for both of us, she was able to hang onto the bow mooring line that was still tied onto our boat, so there was no danger of us drifting away. We were all safe. Sort of, as long as Laurie didn't let go.

After many years of making mistakes like this in various sailboats, I have had my attorney make up a form for accidental situations. The form lists my insurance company, the name and fax number of my insurance agent, his home and work phone number, the limits of liability of my policy, and the name of the law firm that represents me, "BEATEM, BASHEM, BUSTEM AND BREAKEM." On the back of the form there is room for a diagram of the accident and a place for witnesses to describe what I will convince them they have just seen happen.

It's lucky that the young boy on the Bayliner I had crashed into was wearing a life jacket. I had hit his dad's new boat hard enough to knock him into the same ice cold, oily water that my wife was still trying to stay afloat in. His father had wisely purchased a new boat hook with his new Bayliner and was already screaming at everyone within a 1,000 yards to help him fish his kid out from between the four dead sea gulls.

I was now very busy trying to convince his wife that it was their fault because I had hit their starboard side. I got their name and address and they got the I.D. numbers off my boat, California I.D. numbers that had expired several years before.

Through all of this screaming and confusion, the other skipper's mother-in-law had somehow gotten locked in the public toilets and showers. Her paranoidal fear of going on the new Bayliner with her son-in-law as the skipper was only slightly more terrifying than being left behind, locked in a shower that was available to any man or woman for three minutes with four quarters.

While Dad got his son separated from the sea gulls and Mom was going for help to unlock grandma from the public showers, I was fine tuning the rpm on my engine so it would idle just right. By the time I got it adjusted, the gas dock lady was busy throwing the sea gulls back in the water and toweling dry the half-drowned kid. The new skipper of the new Bayliner was looking closely at the nine inch hole I had just carved in the side of his new boat. My wife had somehow managed to climb out of the ice cold, oily, gunk-filled bay and was shivering beside me. She was looking for some gasoline to wash the oily, saltwater from her wet body.

I gave everyone in sight the old thumbs up, eased the throttle forward, and headed slowly east towards the harbor entrance where I would make a slow turn to the north and begin our "Pursuit of Adventure."

As the first chop outside the harbor slapped the hull, my wife was still shivering and already cowering in the cutty cabin, wondering why she said "I do" to me one afternoon years ago. Did the preacher really mean it when he said, "until death do you part?"

Was this going to be the, "until death do us part," part?

LURCHING

Whether you are skiing the powder snow of Colorado or windsurfing off the hot sunny beaches of Maui, it is easy to realize that the world is full of incredible experiences. In between, we spend most of our life lurching from one near disaster to the next, each disaster interrupted occasionally by brief moments of euphoria.

On a cold, crisp, sunny, spring morning recently, I had the pleasure of enjoying one of the few adult toys, a shiny jet airplane, that would almost make me want to be a successful businessman so I could justify owning one of them. (I respect successful businessmen, but I sure have had a lot of fun instead!)

I was headed home after helping raise money for The Mammoth Lakes Foundation, Dave McCoy's project to build a college at Mammoth Lakes, California.

Normally it is a 3 1/2 hour drive from Mammoth to Reno, where I would catch a commercial airliner for Seattle.

If there were one-way rent-a-cars available.

There were none.

The northbound Greyhound bus goes by Mammoth at 1:05 A.M. and arrives in Reno at 5:45 A.M.

When I used to travel and do all of my filming and the live narration of my films, I would have been on that bus and slept every mile of the way. I would have also saved the $6 rental of a motel for the night, and used the money I saved to buy one more roll of film.

My good friend, Dave McCoy's son, Randy, gave me a ride in his dad's Falcon Jet, an over 400 mph, sleek, silent, machine of aluminum, stainless steel, electronics, and grey leather.

I was luxuriating in the grey leather as we lifted off into the early morning sun. We were already going 110 mph and climbing rapidly, while slowly turning to the left to head north towards Reno. We continued to climb up to 22,000 feet, while I talked with Jack Smith, Abby Dalton, and Bob Hart who had gone along with me just for the round-trip jet ride. We talked about the future of the college and Dave McCoy's commitment to the opportunities it would provide the employees of Mammoth, as well as the opportunities for the community.

At 22,000 feet, we leveled off for about four minutes and then started down for a landing in Reno. Instead of a 4:45 bus ride, the jet flight took less than 20 minutes.

Now began the long wait at the Reno International Airport. Here I witnessed a phenomenon that I had never seen before, a floor to ceiling room with glass walls about 12 feet square reserved for smokers only. It would uncomfortably seat ten people and there were 14 people inside of it, sucking enthusiastically on their cigarettes, pipes, and cigars. These people were not lurching from one near-disaster to another; they were in the process of creating their own personal disasters.

47

Through the dense smoke, you could see them all sucking, much the same as a condemned man might, just before the firing squad bullets hit.

Something symbolic here?

The room with 14 smokers in it had air conditioning for three people, and the tobacco smoke was so dense it looked like a foggy moor in an old Alfred Hitchcock movie.

I knew instinctively that these 14 smelly smokers would all be sitting next to me, or very near me, on the flight to Seattle. They smelled like a squad of firemen who had just put out an eleven-alarm fire at the local garbage dump, except for the lady with the tattoos and 14 pounds of quarters that she had taken out of a slot machine just before takeoff. She smelled like cheap perfume and the cigar she had been smoking in the glass room/cage in Reno.

However, her tattoo was spelled correctly.

It's hard to misspell DAD.

The commercial airliner took off and landed at the right rate of speed, which is all I dare ask of any commercial airline today. This one did the first half of its job two and a half hours late.

The next and last leg of my trip home was aboard a float plane from Lake Union in downtown Seattle, to my home in the San Juan Islands. The plane was a De Havilland Beaver that was built in 1957. Its big, ancient, thundering, nine cylinder radial engine supplies the power to pull it through the air at almost 100 mph, an engine so noisy that the pilot has to supply earplugs to all of the passengers.

With a full load of six other paying passengers, I was the heaviest, so I got to sit in the right-hand front seat alongside the pilot. It was a hot, sunny afternoon and sitting behind me were two young boys of about eight or ten years of age. They were heading home from a weekend in the big city with Grandma and Grandpa.

Lifting off from Lake Union, the pilot skillfully dodged the many power boats and managed not to blow over the half a dozen sailboats that looked to me as though they were right in our flight path. The 37-year-old float plane climbed slowly and, at the north end of Lake Union, we had climbed to almost 500 feet, while the pilot nursed it into a slow left turn over the almost ancient, Gas Works Park.

The spring green lawn around the ancient machinery was heavily sprinkled with sprawling, alabaster-white bodies that hadn't been exposed to the sun for many months. (The owner of each white body was desperately trying to be the first one in the office with a tropical tan.) A few of the more athletic white bodies were flying colorful kites that were reaching up to wave hello to us as we slowly flew by just above them.

We then flew west for a few minutes and turned north above Shilshole Marina. I would be home in less than an hour. Or, so I thought.

Remember my lurching from one near disaster to another hypothesis? Twenty minutes after takeoff, the small boy behind me tapped the pilot on the shoulder and, using sign language, conveyed some sort of message of desperation to him. The pilot then motioned for me to remove my earplugs so he could holler to me.

"Mr. Miller, do you mind if we land? The young boy behind you has to go to the bathroom."

What could I say? We were about four miles off shore, and I figured the pilot knew more than I did about this sort of thing. A bumpy water landing in The Straights of Juan De Fuca, midway between Whidbey and Lopez Islands, is a lot better than a messy airplane cabin.

I'm glad the pilot knew what he was doing, as we bounced off the first half dozen waves and finally settled down to become a propeller driven boat, instead of a propeller driven airplane. When the float plane glided to a bobbing stop, the pilot explained to the young boy how to put on his life jacket. Then, he climbed out on the float, opened the cabin door and tied a tether on the youngster and helped him to climb down onto the float.

While the rest of us watched the circling sea gulls, the nine-year-old boy raised the level of Puget Sound by one small bladderfull. He then climbed back up into his seat, took off his life jacket, and buckled up his belt. The pilot locked the cabin door and climbed back into his seat. There, he started throwing switches, and the big, noisy, radial engine once again roared into life.

Gradually gaining speed, we bounced from wave to wave until one of them kicked us into the air and we lifted off to, once again, become an airplane instead of a boat.

Twenty minutes later, we landed (or is it watered?) near a secluded dock on one of the over 400 San Juan Islands. There, my wife met me in our Boston Whaler to take me to our own home on the beach on one of the other islands near the Canadian Border.

I had once again proven my hypothesis of lurching from one near disaster to the next, interrupted by moments of sheer euphoria.

This near-disaster was almost caused by the full bladder of a nine-year-old boy.

Dateline: February, 1968. Sports headlines all over the world read:

JEAN CLAUDE KILLY WINS THREE OLYMPIC GOLD MEDALS SKIING IN FRANCE

August of 1968, after six months of negotiations and pre-production planning, I'm now standing barefooted in my jockey shorts in waist-deep, freezing cold water. We're at a mountain lake at the base of Mt. Ruapehu, on the North Island of New Zealand. I was the only one in the film crew dumb enough to wade out and help nudge a small amphibious plane ashore that is delivering Jean Claude Killy and Leo La Croix to our production crew for the first month of a six month long ski odyssey.

Our original production plans had been to film in Portillo, Chile. Lack of snow made us switch at the last minute to Mt. Ruapehu where I had never personally directed a film before.

And, I have never directed one there since.

The weather in New Zealand was as bad as our accommodations were good. We could sit in the hotel lobby eating lobster pate', fresh trout, or peanut butter and strawberry jam finger sandwiches, while sipping tea and looking out from under the rain clouds to see the sun, always shining four or five miles away. My cameraman, Don Brolin, and my son, Scott, together with a crew of twelve other people, sat around day after day watching it rain, and moped like the professionals we were, while the first episode of our TV show was going way over budget with each passing hour.

Meanwhile, only ten miles away, standing in the bright winter sunshine, the smoking volcano, Narahoe, beckoned to us, "come over and ski and film."

We talked a lot about trying to film skiers skiing its steep wind-blown ridges. That would mean hiking seven miles to the base of the mountain and hauling 100 pounds of camera gear every mile of the way, just to get to the snow line. Once there, we would have to climb for every single shot of every single ski turn.

At about 3:30 on the afternoon of the thirteenth rainy day in a row, while sipping a pot of tea and having one more fresh lobster pate' sandwich in the hotel, Narahoe erupted with a spectacular cloud of smoke and steam, while blowing rocks and ashes downwind as far as twelve miles. Fortunately for us, the prevailing wind was away from the hotel. The hot ashes and rocks, however, left an ugly black slash down the eastern slope that now stood out in sharp contrast to the white snow.

Every afternoon for the next three days, Narahoe violently erupted between 3:30 and 4:00, as though triggered by some accurate geological time clock. By now, we were getting desperate for footage of Jean Claude and Leo doing anything that had to do with skiing.

I began to think,

"Why not try to hire a helicopter that could fly us over to the summit of the volcano early in the morning? We could ski and film until about 3:15. The helicopter could then pick us up somewhere on the side of the mountain and fly us home so we could escape before the scheduled daily volcanic eruption, an eruption which should once again occur on schedule.

The disclaimer is "should."

A pilot was hired and the next morning Don Brolin and I lifted off at 7:30 with the pilot who was wearing a tweed sport coat over a white linen shirt with a button-down collar and a tartan-plaid wool necktie, heavy woolen pants, and brown and white saddle shoes.

This man was no leather gloved, silk scarf, crash helmeted, pilot. He was so confident of his own ability that he was dressed as though he was going downtown to the Saturday night dance. He had made no emergency plans whatsoever for any problem out there, wherever he was going to fly us. This gave us all an immense amount of confidence in his ability as a pilot.

Dumb!

Ten minutes later, he dropped Don and me off on the rim of the smoking volcano and quickly lifted off to bring Jean Claude and Leo up to us on his next trip.

It was truly awesome to stand on the lip of an active volcano and look down into the smoking and steaming crater, to stand there on the ash-covered ice and snow and see pieces of the earth moving around down there. We were almost overpowered by the stench of sulphur dioxide and wondered if it would blow up before we finished filming at 3:30, or while we still stood there.

We had planned on filming on the prevailing windward side of the volcano. That way, if it did blow up while we were up there, the rocks and ashes would blow down the other side of the mountain, instead of falling down on top of us.

I felt safe. Sort of.

We spent all day filming Jean Claude and Leo skiing very aggressively against a background of the smoking crater. We were skiing along the edge of the crater, looking down into the billowing, sulphurous smoke, and recording the roar of whatever was going on, deep down in the bowels of the earth.

About 2:30, the ground began to shake every few minutes with increasingly sharper and more violent earthquakes, so that it was getting difficult to get steady camera shots.

Don and I talked it over and my extensive experience of one semester in college Geology 1-A, made our decision for us.

"I think it'll be an hour before it kicks off its daily explosion."

"Let's go for one last flight to the summit."

When we landed on the volcano's rim this last time, the incredible roar blasting out of the crater had increased to such a volume that it was impossible for anyone to hear my directions when I was shouting a foot away from their ear.

We couldn't even hear the helicopter we were climbing out of.

I had to use sign language.

We all knew that this would be our last filming and skiing descent of Narahoe, so Killy and La Croix really did a number on the available terrain.

For years, I have said,

"Skiing is like dancing with the mountain."

Today, we were all skiing and dancing with death.

During our third camera setup, Don and I looked at each other and then took our cameras off our tripods because the ground was now shaking so much, we couldn't get a steady shot. The last few shots we got of Killy and La Croix, we had to hand-hold our cameras; as they carved turns, they were framed against the growing cloud of steam, sulphur dioxide gas, ashes, and the occasional rocks that were starting to be blasted skyward.

We only needed one last shot of the helicopter landing and picking up Leo and Jean Claude to complete the sequence. I was shocked, though, as I watched it come in for a landing, down below us, and disappear into a dense fog bank. It disappeared at least three miles away from where we were supposed to be picked up, way out in the flat.

My French, by this time, on the trip, had improved to where it was only about 98% sign language and Jean Claude and Leo's English was about the same. We all understood the sign language of survival, though, and the two of them didn't even slow down after the last shot, as they raced right on by us and disappeared in the dense fog, headed for the now distant sound of the helicopter.

Don and I quickly threw our cameras into our rucksacks, tucked our tripods under our arms and followed their ski tracks down to where the brush and trees began to stick up out of the snow. Somehow, Jean Claude had found a path through the underbrush to where the helicopter was waiting. By the time we got there, he and Leo were already strapped in and the pilot motioned to us that he would be back to pick us up in a few minutes.

Let's see, that would mean he would be back about 3:45, about fifteen minutes beyond the volcano's normal explosion time.

I sure hoped the wind would keep blowing from the northwest so, if the volcano did blow up while we were still there, we wouldn't get buried under its daily shower of rocks and ashes. In the thick fog, I don't know how the pilot, who was still wearing his tweed jacket, necktie, and dancing shoes, was going to be able to find us.

He showed up as he said he would, and on time, too. We quickly lashed our skis onto the landing gear and put our tripods and rucksacks full of camera gear on the floor of the small, three-passenger, Bell helicopter, while he adjusted the controls and lifted off. At about 200 feet above the ground, we broke out of the fog and could see the hotel sitting off in the distance, still under a rain cloud. Off to our left, Narahoe's volume of smoke had increased dramatically while we had been nervously waiting in the fog for the chopper's return. The pilot gave us the thumbs up and, just at the same moment, the biggest eruption we had seen in a week blew out of the crater where we had been standing and filming less than 25 minutes earlier.

When the "Jean Claude Killy Skis New Zealand" episode of our new TV series was edited and presented to the networks for approval, their Ethics and Practices Committee made us change it all around. They claimed, "no one would believe the sequence, because no one would be dumb enough to ski down the side of an active volcano."

We were.

And we did.

TRAVELS WITH
JEAN CLAUDE KILLY

In 1968, after the winter Olympics in Grenoble, France, my film company won the assignment of producing a television series featuring Triple Gold Medal winner, Jean Claude Killy. We would be traveling and skiing all over the world, a different country, ski resort, or state every week for 13 weeks. New Zealand, Australia, Mammoth, Vail, Grindelwald, Switzerland, Aspen, Chamonix, St. Moritz, ad exhaustion, ad nauseam. Our first stop had been the North Island of New Zealand on the side of Mt. Ruapehu, where we had a three week bout with bad weather. We finally got enough film in the can by spending some time skiing on a nearby active volcano that was blowing up every day between 3:30 and 4:00 p.m. Once we had such a spectacular sequence completed, we boarded a charter DC-3 for the South Island, to ski on Mt. Cook and the Tasman glacier.

Our DC-3 settled in to land on a field that was just a bumpy strip of grass about 20 miles from the hotel, where the Mt. Cook Airline terminal consisted of a fire extinguisher and a first-aid kit in a wooden box nailed to a four-by-four post. Resting nearby was a set of four stairs mounted on what looked like a pair of wheelbarrow wheels. We taxied to a stop and the co-pilot jumped out and hauled the rolling steps over to the plane so we could all climb out and start unloading our mountain of camera equipment and skis onto the wet grass and mud.

Some time later, as we drove towards the Mt. Cook Hotel, all of the Southern Alps that we wanted to see were shrouded in low hanging clouds. They are a rugged range of snow and glacial-covered mountains that are larger than the Swiss, Austrian, Italian, and French Alps combined. The wind and rain beat incessantly against the overloaded van as we slowly gained altitude. Twenty minutes later, an occasional snowflake was mixed with the torrential downpour, and this was soon followed by wet, sticky snow that forced the ancient windshield wipers to finally grind to a halt.

Here at the base of Mt. Cook, the New Zealand weather, never predictable, once again refused to cooperate with our limited production schedule. With 15 people in our production crew, the Killy TV series was already way over budget because of the rainy three weeks we had already spent on the North Island.

We had only budgeted one week.

Once we bedded down in the Mt. Cook Hotel, we had to again sit and wait in a heavy rain and sleet storm for five long days. During that time, it was coats and ties for lunch and dinner, or they wouldn't even let you into the dining room. After dinner on the fifth night, I took a long walk and was mentally figuring out how much money I was losing by the hour, when the weather suddenly started to clear a bit. By the time I got back to the hotel, The Southern Cross was shining brightly in the middle of a canopy of stars.

I was excited.

Maybe tomorrow?

By this time, we had another small three-place Bell Helicopter standing by. It was flown by a bounty hunter named Mel Cain. The Tasman Glacier is normally out of bounds for helicopter landings, but somehow Mel had managed to get permission for us to land anywhere we wanted to in the Mt. Cook National Park.

I could write an entire book about that one day on the glacier. The foolish chances we took, without a guide. The incredible beauty of a 12 mile long, three mile wide glacier with only four people skiing on it. Turning endlessly in a foot or two of light, untracked, powder snow, with a 1,000 foot base. Hundred foot deep crevasses, that could kill you if you made one mistake. Cobalt blue ice blocks that were 70 feet high and looked as though they would tip over while you were skiing below them.

The helicopter let us out on slopes that were so steep the pilot had to anchor the landing gear in the snow while still hovering. We then had to climb out on that skid, inch our way along it in our ski boots, and gently step off into the hip-deep powder snow, all the while being very careful not to jump off because the sudden loss of weight would make the helicopter tip over and crash. Then we would have to ski down the 12 mile long glacier and hike the last four or five miles back to the hotel in the dark.

We filmed Killy and Lacroix hanging outside, underneath the helicopter, and dropping 40 feet through the air onto untracked powder snow and skiing away. Mt. Cook was off in the distance, in air so clear it looks as though it is less than a mile away, yet it is 12 miles.

How scared I was when, without a guide, I fell part way into a crevasse. When I managed to climb out, I threw a coin down into it and counted the seconds before I heard it hit anything. It was four seconds. I would have died down there and come out of the bottom of the glacier four or five hundred years from now with about 900 feet of exposed, but undeveloped, movie film of Killy and Lacroix skiing.

We lost all track of time while setting up and completing each camera take of the two best skiers in the world.

Collectively, we had more adrenalin flowing among the four of us than most people generate in a lifetime.

It seemed as though only a brief moment had passed since we had started filming at the top of the glacier on the first flight when the light began to fade. There wasn't a cloud in the sky, yet it was getting dark. An entire day had passed. The sun had gone down and we couldn't get any more powder snow and hanging ice block shots.

It wasn't until then that Mel said,

"It's already too late to fly the first two of you out. It'll be pitch dark by the time I can get back up here and try and get the other two. It'll be impossible to find whoever has to wait behind."

His solution to the problem seemed very simple at first. He would let two of us ride inside the helicopter and the other two would get to ride on the outside, tied onto the landing gear. This added up to five people, including the pilot, four pair of skis, and over 100 pounds of camera equipment. That's a big overload trying to take off in a small two passenger, three-place helicopter at about 10,000 feet.

Mel then suggested,

"Why not flip a coin to see who has to ride on the inside and who gets to ride on the outside?"

"Why not?"

But before the coin was flipped, I reminded the group,

"I own the film company." Don, Leo, and Jean Claude could decide who got to ride on the outside."

Don "lost," and he and I had to ride on the inside and Killy and Lacroix got to ride on the outside. In order to do this, we tied two pair of skis, bindings down, on each of the landing skids to make two platforms. We then could tie Killy and La Lacroix to these platforms, on each side of the helicopter. Hurriedly, we tied them onto the skis like two dead deer.

Now it was up to Mel to somehow get this grossly overweight helicopter off the ground, with five people, over 100 pounds of camera gear, and four pair of skis. He revved the engine up until the tachometer screamed against the red line. The machine began to respond by struggling, almost desperately, until it finally got a few feet off the snow, where it hovered for a brief moment and came back down with a thud! Mel then fine tuned a couple of the controls, and gave the engine a little different mixture of fuel and air. This time, it was able to fly up four or five feet in the air, hover for about five seconds, and come down gently.

After four or five of these four foot high flights, I noticed that Mel was kind of leapfrogging his way, slightly downhill, to the left. He was flying about 15 or 20 feet horizontally with each jump.

Concerned, I shouted,

"Why are you heading this way?"

Mel hollered back,

"There's a cliff over there. I'm trying to time my short flights so that, when we get close to the edge, we'll be airborne and can fall off of it so I can get air speed. Once we do that, we can hopefully maintain enough forward air speed so I can get all of us back to the hotel."

Hopefully, was the disclaimer I didn't like.

But somehow he timed it right, and we did.

That night at dinner, Killy said it the way it really is.

"A mountain is like a beautiful woman. You can go to her as often as you want, but she will only give you whatever she wants."

"Today, she gave us our lives."

"Mel was leap-frogging the helicopter towards the cliff so we could fall off and gain air speed."

COMMUNICATION

Webster defines communication as "information transferred, a verbal or written message."

At a well known ski resort everyone was speaking English, and yet it was difficult to believe that they were trying to do what Webster defines as communication. Here are some examples.

SNOWBOARDERS

"It was like it was really awesome man. It was like that dude was trying to go backside when, like that freaky old guy on a pair of sleds, like cut him off and he had to do, like a knee spread slide spinner."

PRIVATE SKI INSTRUCTOR

"That was without a doubt the most beautiful turn I have ever seen executed by one of my pupils in the many years I have been teaching. Your right hand was in just exactly the right position, clenched firmly around your ski pole."

"Your knees were bent just right so they gave a beautiful drape to your ski outfit."

"Your shoulders were hunched just enough to give a semblance of speed."

"Your overall body position was bent just enough at the waist to match the prescribed perfect 12% from the vertical plane so that the side camber of your skis worked exactly right throughout the entire arc of that well executed turn."

"Now if you would like a week of private lessons, I can in all probability elevate your ski ability to where you can possibly become good enough to win a bronze Nastar medal."

(And I can buy my spousal equivalent a new fur coat with what you are going to have to pay me for the week of racing lessons.)

"I can see it now, the certificate framed in your office, and you wearing the medal proudly on that red, yellow, blue, green, and beige ski suit."

"What do you say?"

SKI SALESMAN

"The side camber of this imported French Giant Slalom beauty is made of carbon fibers and stainless steel and is 1.83 millimeters more extreme than last month's model. That one, as you probably know, allowed the manufacturer to put 11% more torsional rigidity in this new, high speed cruising model. On top of all that, don't you think the new cosmetics would look just darling with your new 47 zipper, grey and yellow, powder snow, ski suit?"

WEATHERMAN

"When we incorporate the adiabatic lapse rate into the descending jet stream as it flows over the Continental Divide, we will have 19% of the moisture contained in it, condense around the smog molecules that were acquired as the air mass descended low over Los Angeles. All of these interlocked variables may just let us see as much as an inch and a quarter of sparkling white, wind-driven snow by a week from next Saturday."

SKI BOOT SALESMAN

"This model is made of semi-elasticized polymer. It has been homogenized with approximately 14% of catalyzed fiberglass at 117 degrees Fahrenheit with a 3% humidity factor in the oven as it is strategically superimposed around the ankle bone to give you 19% more lateral stability when you are skiing in densely wooded areas with a light intensity of f 5.6. This, as you of course already know, when combined with a highly flexible, longitudinally, however, stiff laterally yet semi-soft polymer foot bed with a built in extension cord for your boot heaters will now allow you to walk back and forth from the bus to the ski lift a lot more comfortably."

FUR COAT SALESMAN

"With each fur coat we sell, we furnish a certificate of suicide for each animal that gave its life to make the creation of this beautiful coat something that you just cannot live without."

SNOWCAT DRIVER

"If I hit the throttle a little harder and lower the blade two extra inches and elevate the grinder a mere eleven degrees just below this road, I can make the rocks come almost to the surface of the snow and they will still be invisible to anyone skiing down until they get some air when they hit the road."

SNOWBOARD COSTUME SALESPERSON

"With this outfit that I just acquired from the overweight father of a family of street people in Little Rock, you will be able to cover up that beautiful 36-24-36 body of yours so you can look like a sack of trash on the way to the dump. If you put your hair up in this size twelve baseball hat, wear it backwards and don't wear any makeup, you exactly match the description of that robber that hit the Seven-Eleven last night."

"Tell that dude in the car that we just got a new brand of sunblock in stock. It has fine, decomposed, dark granite in it, so he will look like he hasn't shaved for at least four days."

"And with each new rad snowboard outfit, I'll give you like a free map of where all the cowabanga bumps and like the gnarly rad cliffs are."

RESORT MARKETING DIRECTOR

"When we go into that particular foreign market and maximize our penetration with a substantially financed print blitz, backed with a television and radio saturation buy, we will in all probability, acquire our share of the existing ski market away from the other resorts in the same geographical marketing area, which, of course, is worldwide. We will have to have our esoteric message translated into the proper native language idiomatic expressions that will add another 5% to our overall marketing budget. If we don't translate idiomatically, those potential customers might get the wrong message and think that we claim to offer better skiing than anywhere else."

SKI BINDING SALESMAN

"This new triple-cam model, with the interior adjustable sensing cam operated release mechanism and the automatically adjusting sole thickness Tetonic plate will let you get in and out of your skis at the end of every run more easily. That way, you can have another cup of coffee or visit the restroom without even bending over to release the heel of your boot. And speaking of boot heels, this patented binding is so simple that I have been told that the Boeing

Aircraft Company is going to replace all of the buckles in all of their airplane seatbelts with this new, revolutionary model."

"And, it releases so quickly that the Archer Daniels Midland Company is marketing a slight variation of it to the farmers in the Midwest as the rat trap of the future."

"Ah, I see I have coerced you into buying a set of them. Just step over there and the cashier will see if you still have enough float left on your credit card."

Now, that's communication!

"Nice transition."

ABOUT CHAIRLIFTS

The chairlift on Ruud Mountain at Sun Valley in 1947, had a very peculiar characteristic. It ran as though it had a mind of its own. If you didn't sit down gently when you started your ride, and jumped on instead, this would start the cable bouncing a little bit. If this happened, you were in for a big surprise as you got closer to the first tower. That first tower had been built just exactly the wrong distance from where you boarded the lift. Through some unique mathematical equation of time versus distance, a very rare type of rapidly increasing, harmonic vibration was set up. Your small initial bounce was rapidly magnified in height until, just before you got to that "built in the wrong place" first tower, you were thrown unceremoniously and violently out of the chair. You would then land in the snow 20 feet below. This would only happen in front of your friends. Even after you learned of this chairlift's mechanical idiosyncrasy, trying to hang on each time you made a mistake getting on was nearly impossible. This was, after all, only the second or third chairlift built in the world and engineering knowledge, mixed with contemporary ski techniques, weren't all that sophisticated.

Until 1936, when they invented the chairlift, one of the few ways you could get a real thrill out of skiing was to be a Nordic ski jumper. For each jump, you would have to spend at least half an hour climbing up to the top of the hill, or in-run, with your thick, wide, heavy, eight foot long skis over your shoulder. There, you'd rest a bit, put 'em on, and then start down the in-run, gaining as much speed as the hill allowed, until you flew, or jumped off the lip. Depending on the height of the hill, the object was always to go far enough through the air as possible to come in for a gentle landing at a tangent to the steep landing hill.

Nordic jumping was most popular in the Midwest, where the hills are not very high. At most of the locations, ski clubs would spend every summer weekend building a scaffold for their new, bigger, higher in-run, way up above the top of the landing hill. The agony of climbing, the shakiness of the scaffolds built out of scrounged lumber, and the lack of safety bindings kept most people from ever becoming ski jumpers.

Smart people.

This began to change in 1936, when the chairlift was invented by a Union Pacific Railroad engineer. Skiing immediately began to come of age because, at the same time, the railroad also invented Sun Valley, Idaho. Now, you could finally ski downhill all day long and never have to climb back up. Just sit down in a moving chair and be hauled back up for as many rides as your strength, skill, and money allowed. All of this for only a couple of dollars a day.

When it was decided to build Sun Valley, one of the first memos written by Averill Harriman, president of the railroad, called for "mechanical devices to take people to the tops of the slides." Engineers in Omaha, Nebraska, home base of the railroad, immediately went to work on variations of the already invented rope tow (1934), and the J-Bar (1935).

A young railroad engineer named Jim Curran, who had helped build equipment for loading bananas on fruit boats in the tropics, was a member of the railroad team who were assigned the task. To him, transporting skiers or bunches of bananas, without bruising them, presented much the same problem. The only difference was the temperature in which they were transported. All Jim did was simply replace the banana hooks that hung from a moving cable, with chairs.

His original drawings were almost overlooked in the first presentation to Averrill Harriman; but former Olympic skier, Dartmouth ski coach, and consultant, Charlie Proctor, spotted the drawings and sent them on to Harriman with his recommendations,

"Curran's ideas are the best. Let him design and build the whole thing!"

By July, a mock-up of the chair was built in the bed of a pickup truck in a hot railroad yard in Omaha, Nebraska. A bunch of timbers resembling half of a T were hung out over the side of the truck. Hanging from this structure was a free swinging, two inch in diameter, piece of pipe. The chair seat was welded to the bottom of the pipe and was the same distance off the ground as a normal chair with legs. Jim Curran's engineering team thought that they could drive the pickup truck with the chair facing forward and scoop up a waiting-in-line skier. Driving the truck at a variety of speeds, they could eventually decide on which speed was the best, and fastest, to scoop up waiting skiers without injuring them.

"With a few modifications, this'll revolutionize the ski lift business."

Time was beginning to run out by the time they got their contraption built and ready for testing. Whatever uphill device they came up with had to be invented, designed, engineered, built, tested, and hauling paying passengers on the side of a hill in the remote wilds of Idaho by Christmas. They had less than five months left to complete the entire job. A decision on final design had to be made quickly, so expert skier, John E.P. Morgan, was summoned to Omaha to test this revolutionary new idea. He arrived with skis, boots, poles, and wearing warm, woolen ski clothes. He looked, and had to feel, pretty silly standing around, sweating, amidst the steam engines and a handful of railroad engineers involved in a top secret project. At first, E.P. Morgan simply stood on a pile of straw as the truck drove by slowly and tried to scoop him up. Straw proved not to be slippery enough, as John picked himself up from the cinder-covered railroad yard a few dozen times.

At lunch, someone suggested,

"Why not add some oil to the straw?"

They did, and now John had oily straw stuck to the bottom of his skis and it didn't slide very well either.

But it sure made a lot more of that oil-saturated straw stick to his clothes every time he fell.

Then a junior engineer suggested,

"Let's try a pair of roller skates. There's some concrete out by the roundhouse that we can drive back and forth on."

A couple of hours later, with John E.P. Morgan in his thick woolen, winter ski clothes, sweating profusely, the maximum speed of loading live bodies on the, as yet unnamed, tramway was finally decided, a speed, incidentally, that is still being used in chairlifts all over the world today.

The engineers now started working around the clock until all of the working drawings were completed. Construction on the various parts was begun in the railroad machine shop as fast as they were designed. Most of them were built railroad-strong in those Omaha shops. While this was progressing, some of the engineering crew rode the train out to Sun Valley to get "The Tramway" under construction.

As the *Hailey Weekly* newspaper said, "To carry ski jumpers up to where they will shoot back down."

Today, the American Society of Tramway Safety Engineers probably wouldn't let that first-ever-built-ski-lift operate, because of its lack of safety devices.

But, let me tell you a little more about its design.

The lift towers were single, wooden poles that could easily double for telephone poles. The cross 'T' that supported the wheels, or sheaves, that the cable ran over was at least made of metal. The sheaves, or wheels, were also metal so that, every time the grip that the chair was attached to the cable with bumped over the metal sheaves, your chair and you got a real jolt.

Fortunately, it wasn't a double chairlift because the ride was so noisy that you never could have heard anything your partner was saying.

In the summer of 1936, there was no such thing as a tractor that could climb Dollar Mountain to haul all of the materials up to erect the new Tramway. The parts were hauled up by pack mule or on the backs of ten cent an hour, out-of-work miners.

While it was under construction, Sun Valley's publicity genius, Steve Hannigan, gave this remote Idaho Tramway a new name that is as famous today as the ski itself. Steve coined the name "Chairlift."

It was completed on time, on budget, for the grand Christmas opening. However, there was no reason for anyone to ride it until after the arrival of the first snowfall, which didn't show up until January ninth. Once the snow arrived in the Valley, the Dollar lift started running without a problem.

It had been made railroad-strong.

My first experience with that "first in the world, ski lift" according to my diary, was on January 27, 1947, when a very attractive young lady invited me for lunch at the Dollar Mountain Cabin. I didn't know it when I accepted the date, but the cabin was at the top of the lift. I didn't want to miss my luncheon date, but I couldn't afford a $4 lift ticket to get up there. (I had already figured out the Mt. Baldy lift operator manipulation system so I could ride those lifts without a ticket.) So, I did the next best thing. I arrived at the base of Dollar an hour early, climbed to the top of the mountain and skied over to the sun porch of the Dollar Cabin. I enjoyed the great lunch and my date's Texas accent. After lunch, Josephine Abercrombie and her girlfriend, Audrey Beck, seemed to be content to just lean back and soak up the sun, so I took a calculated risk. I climbed into my skis, waved good-by for awhile, and skied down the west ridge of the Dollar Bowl in beautiful, untracked powder snow. At the bottom, I skied right up to get back on the lift as though I had been riding it all day.

"Can I see your lift ticket please?"

"Oh! I left it on my parka. It's hanging up on the sun deck at the restaurant at the top."

"Be sure to bring it down next time."

"Sure, I will."

I didn't have a parka, so I looked around the sun deck at the top, spotted one with a lift ticket hanging on it, found out who owned it, and said to the owner,

"I'm really cold; could I borrow your parka and make a few runs wearing it?"

The guy who loaned it to me was really busy trying to hustle my date and sipping Dom Perignon, while soaking up the sun's warm rays right alongside the two ladies from Texas. I skied four or five runs with that borrowed season lift ticket. Each time at the bottom of the lift, I chatted for a few minutes with the lift operator about his old days on the railroad, his farm in Hailey, how his herd of cows was doing, how early he had to get up to milk all of them to be here in time to start the lift, how many kids he had, where he was born, how hard he worked, important stuff like that.

By the fifth run, that lift operator invited me down to have dinner at his farmhouse some night soon and he knew me so well, he never asked to see my lift ticket again for the rest of the winter. At the top, on the fifth run, I gave the parka back to the man I had borrowed it from and skied free the rest of the day with Josephine and Audrey.

I was virtually guaranteed free lift rides when, a week or so later, I had dinner at the lift operator's farmhouse and met his incredibly beautiful daughter. He told me that he really appreciated it when I didn't make a pass at her. The retired railroad engineer, now Hailey farmer and lift operator, said,

"Warren, as long as I'm taking tickets, you can ski free on Dollar for the rest of the winter."

More ski lift history.

In 1948, Sun Valley management decided to build a new chairlift up the ridge between the two Dollar Bowls, in order to open up more ski terrain. How word of tearing down old ski lifts spreads, I don't know. Even in '48, there wasn't much of a market for a 12-year-old chairlift. However, a man who would later design, build, and own the best ski resort in the Midwest heard about it being for sale. Driving out from Boyne Mountain, Michigan, in a flatbed truck, Everett Kercher brought with him his new ski school director, Victor Gottchalk.

It took Everett a couple of days to negotiate the final price of the lift with Pappy Rogers, the general manager of Sun Valley. Pappy had a price in his mind that Everett thought was unconscionable. Pappy wanted $5,200 for it, as is, where is. But Everett finally beat him down to $4,800.

As soon as Everett's check cleared the bank, Pappy Rogers let him get to work.

He and Victor got busy with their spanner wrenches and spent the next two weeks dismantling the world's first chairlift. Piece by piece, the two of them loaded it onto their truck and hauled it down to the Ketchum railroad siding, where they loaded it onto a flatbed railroad car. They then climbed into their truck with a full load of stuff and drove back to Boyne Mountain, Michigan. The bull wheels, the large wheels at the top and bottom of the chairlift that the cable changes direction around, turned out to be very large in diameter. While driving their truck back to Michigan Everett and Victor redesigned the single chairlift into a double. The bull wheels were large enough in diameter to keep the cable far enough away from the lift towers so the chairs could carry two people at a time. They even added a new, radical design of rubber-tired sheaves on the towers so the ride up would be quieter. What I liked most about the rubber-tired wheels was that you didn't bounce twice every time you went over every tower.

A few years ago, when I last rode that old Number One lift at Boyne Mountain, Michigan, the upper and lower bull wheels and the original gears from the engine that drove the lower bull wheel shaft in 1936, in Sun Valley, were still "carrying skiers up to where they will shoot back down." That's over 50 years after it was invented in Omaha, Nebraska, by a group of engineers who had never skied a day in their lives.

They built that lift railroad-strong and the basic design of that first chairlift has worked perfectly since it first scooped up E.P. Morgan, on his roller skates, on a hot July afternoon in Omaha, in 1936.

ANTICIPATION

Anticipation always has three different points of view.

1. What you think it will be like.
2. What your friends tell you it will be like.
3. What it is really like.

Let's take a look at some of the things that occur in the ski sport and examine them from all three sides.

On the radio, the ski resort broadcasts,

THE FIRST SNOWFALL OF THE SEASON

You think it will be four feet of light powder snow on top of well mown grass.

Your friends tell you it will be just like it was that day you spent in your car in the parking lot because it was raining so hard you couldn't get across the parking lot.

In reality, the snowfall is a figment of the imagination of the marketing director who was thrown out of Dartmouth for cheating on his creative writing exam.

YOUR FIRST TRIP TO MT. MAGNIFICENT

You think they will have 43 quad chairlifts, countless restaurants, deep powder snow, good looking ski instructors, plenty of groomed runs, and a place where you can get private snowboard lessons. If you're young enough to want them, and rich enough to afford them!

Your friend tells you that she went there and met the most darling ski instructor who helped her on and off the lift for only $425 a day plus a 15% tip. The restaurant she liked the best was where they had line dancing and she managed to dance there four nights in a row before her cowboy boots started to give her blisters. The restaurant at the top of some mountain she couldn't remember the name of had the most divine Buffalo Burgers and don't worry about the cost because you are on a vacation. Make sure you take at least four $20's, if you are going to have a luncheon companion.

It is really so efficient that they have 63 snowcats, so every skiable acre of the mountain is groomed before the sun comes up. The many Fur Salons are having an end-of-season, 70% discount sale two days after the season starts. Private ski lessons are $425 a day and the instructor you get will only speak Lithuanian, but that's O.K. because you've only hired him so you don't have to stand in the two minute lift lines on the many quad chairlifts.

CONDO OWNERSHIP

It will be available whenever the snow is perfect and the sun is out. It will be located in a ski in, ski out location, your friends will only show up when invited a month or more in advance, and the rental agency will fill it up enough so that you make money on it every year.

Your friends warn you of fraternity renters who will trash it, roofs that will leak, rental agencies that won't rent it unless you pay them on the side, and the ski in, ski out is only after a ten minute bus ride.

It is really a place for all of your friends to freeload, and your business acquaintances to use whenever you aren't. The roof will leak and the plumbing will freeze while you are on your

Winter Cruise to the Caribbean. The rental agency has lined up a great contractor to fix it (their immigrant cousin, Manuel) and he only charges eleven times what it would cost you to fix the same problem when there is no snow on the roof.

While you are using your condo, you are either fixing everything that has been broken by your rentors, or cooking endless meals for all of your freeloading friends.

Probably both of the above.

However, there is that occasional Monday when it has been raining for a week and finally snows all Sunday afternoon and night. Monday morning, the road up to Mt. Magnificent is closed because there is two feet of new powder snow.

You are the only person in the lift line because you have a ski in, ski out condo and you didn't read the sign in the base lodge down the road that says the mountain will be closed until noon because of avalanche danger.

SKI MOVIES

You have never seen a ski movie before and your new girlfriend drags you to a Warren Miller ski movie in October. You think you will be sitting on a metal folding chair amongst a handful of Granola eaters, watching a scratched 16mm movie on the floor of a basketball court at the YMCA.

Your friends have never seen one, so they have no opinion.

In reality you watch it while sitting in a reserved seat in a $78 million theater in Orange County with 3,100 other screaming and shouting ski nuts.

"Quit worryin'. I found a place where we can
scare the bejeepers out of our classes."

You walk out of it after having had the same experience you had when you were a sailor and watched a porno film on your ship when it was still four days out of port.

You could watch it, but you couldn't do it.

NEW SKIS

You think they will be the magic for your feet that will have you leaping off tall cliffs, carving beautiful turns in untracked powder snow, and winning the local ski races. All of this for only $679, plus bindings and tuning.

Your friends will tell you that you bought the wrong skis.

You need the new cutting edge technology. Cap skis with high performance tuning done by that guy who used to tune the skis of one of the World Cup racers. You know that famous guy, what's-his-name? And besides, the new cosmetics are a better contrast to your powder suit.

They are really a quantum leap forward and it is a shame that your ski ability is not up to handling the nuances of such a high performance ski. If you were a better skier, you could jump off high cliffs on any ski, you would need fat skis to carve turns in deep powder snow, and you couldn't win a local race on Alberto Tomba's skis.

LIFT LINES

You are a bachelor, watching a beautiful lady climbing into her skis and then slipping off her gloves and removing her wedding ring while skating into the lift line hollering,

"Single!"

You think she is trying to decide whether or not she wants to go back to Fresno and resume her life on the raisin farm with Clyde.

Your friends tell you she will ski with you and, later in the day, accept your dinner invitation while spending all of your money. After dinner, when you walk her to her condo, she will introduce you to her three brothers who are all attorneys.

She is really a ski instructor on her day off. During the summer, she put on ten pounds and her wedding ring is too tight to wear when she is pounding down through the moguls.

LUNCH ON TOP OF THE MOUNTAIN

You think it will be a greasy hamburger and fries, just like it was two or three years ago, and you can get out for $5, including a cup of coffee.

Your friends will probably tell you the same thing unless they have been there.

It is really a sit down, four course elegant meal of Caesar salad, Steak Tartar, Antelope Pasta, White Asparagus from France, chilled Poully Fuisse, and, for dessert, flaming brandy over fresh strawberries and homemade ice cream. The meal takes two and a half hours and your credit card is refused because you don't have high enough limits on it.

Whichever point of view <u>you</u> experience, skiing lives up to its anticipation!

WALNUT SKIS

The multimillion dollar quad chairlifts swing gently in the afternoon breeze. Here and there is a small remaining patch of snow where the winter winds made the drifts deep enough for you to occasionally get some air.

The nubile bodies that have been covered all winter with baggy $1,000 powder suits are now revealed in all of their sensuality by string bikinis stretched out on a million different beach towels on a thousand beaches from Maui to Cape Hatteras.

It is the time of the year to pause and plan for what might come next.

I sit here in my studio working on the script for next year's feature ski film and one sequence stands out dramatically from anything we have ever committed to film before.

No, it is not a world's record cliff jump, it is not someone winning an Olympic Gold medal by three one hundredths of a second, nor is it a brand new ski resort.

It is about the skiing children in a small village in India tucked up against the Tibetan border. It is a summer resort called Manali, a place where the English used to go during the summer to get away from the 130 degree heat of New Delhi. These kids live in a village nearby named Solang, which is located at about 8,000 feet, with apple and walnut orchards all around its perimeter. The average family income is two to three dollars a month. However, it is a village without poverty and a village where they don't need or want what you and I take for granted in order to have fun skiing. They have never seen a rope tow, much less a chairlift.

They do have a broken down poma lift that last ran five or six years ago. Their coach told our camera crew that the kids sometimes climb to 15,000 feet and ski down.

At 15,000 feet, these little kids are getting less than 10% of the oxygen that you and I get at sea level.

And their ski equipment has to be seen to be believed.

Their skis are about 30 to 40 inches long, an inch and a half thick, three inches wide and are made out of a single piece of walnut. That's right, walnut. It is the only wood that is available locally that is strong enough. Apple wood is much too brittle. A pair of 35 inch long skis are as stiff as an iron bar of the same size. Ski boots? They ski in soft rubber goulashes and their bindings are made from woven vines threaded through a hole in the skis.

They have been able to somehow get old, worn out band saw blades from the local saw mill for their metal edges. They then cut the blade about five inches longer than the ski. The extra five inches of the saw blade are bent up to form the tip of the ski. This old piece of band saw blade is then screwed to the bottom of the piece of walnut. The width of the band saw blade dictates the width of the ski. One edge of the ski is smooth and works quite well. The other edge of the ski still has the band saw blade teeth. The kids don't even bother to file them off.

They just have to be extra careful when turning on that side of their skis.

Ski poles are just that. Poles. They just cut a straight sapling and trim off the branches. There is no such thing as a handle or a basket and there was not one single pair of gloves amongst the hundred or more kids who turned out for the filming.

Their jackets were all the same color and the same size. It is as though all of the unsold 1958 Nehru jackets wound up in this village of Solang.

These young boys and the one girl who was allowed to ski with them jump off the roofs of houses, make a credible Wedlen turn, and have a mass start downhill that is something to behold.

The first prize in the weekly downhill was a bicycle inner tube. Quite a valuable prize because the winner could cut it up and use it to make a better, more modern set of ski bindings, instead of his regular bindings of woven vines.

The most impressive part of the group of young skiers to me was the size of their smiles.

They don't need, or want, what you and I take for granted: that which we have to have, so we can have a good time skiing.

Think about the size of their smiles the next time you complain about waiting three minutes in a high speed quad lift line while you are wearing the latest, greatest, and most fashionable ski equipment, or if you have to stand in line for that deluxe lunch at the mountaintop restaurant. Remember, these kids' families have an annual income of between $20 and $35 dollars.

There are no words in the Manali dialect for snow grooming, quad chairlifts, safety bindings, monocoque construction, or man-made snow. But, there are at least a dozen words that all translate to the same, simple three letter word:

FUN.

As you search for that exotic ski vacation location in the travel brochures and clothing and equipment catalogs while you are lying on your beach towel somewhere watching your alabaster-white body slowly turning bright sunburned red, think about the kids of Solang, and whether or not you will have as much fun as they do when you get to your dream destination.

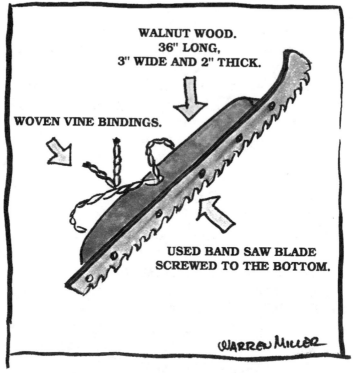

"The Solang powder snow ski."

ARTICLES I'M GLAD I NEVER WROTE ABOUT BOATING

I like being on the water and have spent a lot of my life on boats. I feel I know something about them, and although I still have a lot to learn, I'm glad I knew enough not to submit some of these articles to boating magazines:

Fiberglass: Is it Here to Stay?
There's a Bimbo Under Your Bimini
Down the Inland Waterway the Easy Way:
     Use Someone Else's Boat
Inflatable Dinghy Repair Made Easy
Privacy Curtains Aren't
Fiberglass Blisters, a Fun Summer Project
Boat Designing for the Non-Creative
Ferro Cement: the Boat Manufacturing
     Material of the Future
Bird Dropping Removal with Panache
Stainless Steel Props and Chopped Liver
Planing Speed in Your Sailboat with Twin
     Inboards
The Lost Art of Making Fiddle Blocks
Varnishing Can Be Fun
Getting an Angle on Trim Tabs
Selecting the Proper Bikini to Support Your
     Cellulite
Bronze Sheave Blocks for the Beginner
Rowing a Boat Can be Sweaty
Inland Waterways Can Be Dangerous
What Not to Name Your Boat

Inexpensive Marinas Can Be Old
Is Steam the Power of the Future?
Pitfalls of Improper Tax Deductions for
        Your Boat
Learn Navigation the Easy Way: Buy an
        Airplane Ticket
Fiberglass Resin Removal From Body Parts
Extending the Range of your Electric Launch
How to Convert Your Fish Well Into a Hot Tub
Big Game Fishing Reels for the Reel Beginner
Designing Diving Boards for Swim Steps
Docking for the Dumb
Inflatable Air Bags for Docking Your Boat
Adjustable Steering for the Overweight
Boats that Claim to Sleep Six, Don't
How to Make the Guest Bed Lumpy
Trim Tabs for the Overweight
Folding Ladders for Fun
Empty Beverage Holders Can Be Dangerous
Life Jackets for Live-Aboards
Loud Hailers are for Whimps
Davit Operation for the Uncoordinated
How to Macrame Your Spray Dodger
High Resolution Radar for the Slow Boat
How to Adjust Your Adjustable Table
Anchor Hauling by Muscle, Not Brains
Adjustable Helm Chairs for the Overweight
Bottom Cleaning for the Beginner
Boat Yard Repair Rate Interpretation
Lifeboat Navigation for the Unlucky

APRIL POINT

In search of the wily salmon in their lair, we have towed our spacious yacht about 150 miles north of its home port of Anacortes, Washington. Actually, our boat's home port is on top of a ten year old galvanized iron trailer. Our spacious yacht is a 20 foot PURSUIT, with a 175 hp Johnson on the back, so it can cruise comfortably in the 25 mph range.

We are going to rendezvous with some friends in two days, but we left port early because I have a habit of making lots of mistakes and winding up on the wrong side of an island, or up a sound somewhere. With a lot of luck, I will be low on gas and have to inch our way to the next gas dock on our auxiliary 15 hp Johnson at two knots. It will probably be only about 20 miles to the next gas dock, an excruciating ten hour trip.

At April Point, I'm surprised at the high cost of renting a fishing guide and his 16 foot Boston Whaler that is four feet shorter than my well founded yacht. At $50 an hour, we decided to go alone to the famed fishing grounds. For $50 an hour, you can hire a plumber who will show up at your house without the right tools. What makes you think your guide will have the right fishing lures?

"It's too overcast."

"It's too sunny."

"The gnarly gnat is swarming and the fish are full of natural food so they aren't biting."

"They are four days away, up (or down) coast, so stick around; when we finish with all of our high budget fishermen with reservations, we can take you out. If they haven't caught all the fish that will be off Cape Mudge by then."

My wife, Laurie, and I are milling around off the Cape Mudge lighthouse. And I use the word milling with reservation because, in reality, the normal rocking and rolling of our yacht has been replaced with twirling and swirling in the whirlpools of the nine knot, outgoing tide that is draining half of the Inland Passage to Alaska.

All around us, the April Point guides and their yellow slickered, red plaid, wool shirted customers are sweating in the abnormal August sun. Laurie and I are in our normal bathing suits because it is the natural thing to do in a boat when the sun is out, the convertible top is down, and it is hot. Besides no one told us, just because this is British Columbia, we had to dress like a couple of born deer hunters in a small boat.

Everyone in the dozens of boats around us is deadly serious about this fishing stuff so, of course, they won't tell you how deep to fish or what they have on for bait. I think the high paying fishing guided customers are all being guided to a skin diver who is grabbing their lines and attaching salmons of various sizes from an underwater cage.

And us?

We fished at various depths. Three arm's length pulls of line off the reel, six pulls, ten, four, seven pulls. Still nothing happened except we both got dizzy and mad, as boat after boat drifted by hollering, "Outta' the way." "Under." "Over." "Around." "Got a double."

After a couple of hours of rocking, rolling, and twirling around we are saying, "Well, at least we don't have to clean anything when we get back," when socko, Laurie was hooked onto something big.

Since we are the only boat out of the 150 that are spinning around while fishing this particular whirlpool without $50 an hour guides, we are also the only ones trying to figure out what to do with a four foot long, 20 pound mud shark.

We now have our limit of mud sharks. The gear is put away and we head north for the supermarket at Campbell River for my weekly stash of bologna and peanut butter before we head for April Point Marina.

Campbell River is a good jumping off place from Vancouver Island. You can drive there in your car with a ferryboat ride and a wet map north of Vancouver B.C.

Laurie returned from the Overwaitea Supermarket with enough groceries to stock a boat twice our size. (Editor's note: How would you like to be the marketing director for the *Overwaitea* Supermarkets?) She completely filled two shopping carts. They don't let you take the shopping carts down the 400 yard long dock because too many people take the easy way out and just shove them over the edge of the dock after they empty them, instead of returning them to the store.

During my five trips down the dock to our spacious 20 foot yacht with the 314 bags of groceries, the local fishermen I had to walk by thought they had seen it all. When I walked by with the two potted plants Laurie bought for the instrument panel, they knew they had seen it all. Next time we go boating, I'm going to take along a skateboard with a two foot square sheet of plywood to stack the groceries on.

Our 20 foot yacht is a little light on instruments. We have a fuel gauge and a compass that I had left over from my sailboat racing days. What else do you need? You are either low on gas or out of it, on course or lost, afloat or aground. Nothing else matters. Unless it is too foggy, or too windy. Then you just sit at anchor or at the dock and wait it out.

Laurie has found a treasure in the supermarket, a rare volume of "Living off the Land in British Columbia."

"Over 3,000 recipes to cook anything that crawls, swims, or flies in B.C. after you catch it." Always a disclaimer. "After you catch it."

As we cruise across the Strait towards April Point Marina, we are both disappointed when Laurie can't find a single recipe for mud shark, fried, broiled, boiled, or barbecued.

Any serious western practitioner of the art of, "My boat is bigger than your boat" has to spend some time in this Canadian marina. Dockside reservations are a must. Conspicuous places to tie up, where everyone can walk by "your boat" and see how "Bristol clean" it is, are hard to come by. Real choice dock space, I am told, is reserved as many as three years in advance. Ninety-five foot Hatteras, 57 foot Rybovichs, and a six-pack of cruising together 45 foot Bayliners are lined up like a fleet of avenging warships ready to fight off the invading summer tourists.

Yes, there is even the converted World War II, 110, wooden hulled, Sub Chaser, Cairdeas, with some genuine movie stars on board.

I didn't know enough to phone ahead for reservations, so there isn't any room at the dock even for our 20 foot Pursuit. I've never made a reservation for anything in my life. The 95 foot ChrisCraft owner graciously said he would haul the Pursuit (with us in it, persumably?) aboard his boat for the night, but my yacht might not fit the chocks for his tender.

Laurie and I have spent a lot of nights at anchor and a lot of time talking "aw shucks, we didn't know that" with marina operators. So, it is no big deal for us to get to tie up at the shore boat dock for what is supposed to only be 20 minutes. We take leisurely turns repacking the gear in our Pursuit while one of us walks up to the marina office for a $1.50, Canadian, hot shower.

On my shower shift, I took along our five gallon Gatorade water jug. When I got back with 40 pounds or so of fresh water and a clean body, Laurie had made up a pot of great chowder using the clams we had gathered that morning at low tide on a sandbar near Heriot Bay. The smell of her wonderful clam chowder mixed with the hissing of our Coleman camp stove on the back of our boat was turning a lot of heads as the evening martini set was wandering up and down the dock.

It is almost 10:00 by the time we have expanded our waists three inches in circumference on the clam chowder and fresh french bread from the Overwaitea Supermarket. Time to start up the 175 hp outboard, drive around the end of the dock, and anchor out in the center of the inlet. I'm being very careful to remember that because of the 18 foot tidal change in this part of the world, I always anchor fore and aft so the boat won't swing the length of the anchor line and be on the rocks or in the mud in the morning.

Laurie and I both enjoy bedding down to the sounds of a Marina when we are just far enough away to hear the murmurs, but none of the absolute sounds. We don't get drawn into trying to figure out the bits and pieces of the conversations that go on, as the games people play afloat begin to go adrift.

One of the many pleasures of cruising on a small boat is that sometime during the night you get to bypass the chemical toilet and tinkle over the side, disturbing the millions of planktons or whatever it is that lights up when you disturb them with your midnight tinkle. Ten billion, zillion, fireflies dance and play in The Inland Passage to Alaska because of one emptying bladder.

We are both lifted out of bed by the roar of an airplane engine as the 7:30 A.M. Kenmore Air float plane misses our antenna by nine feet with his left float.

We have anchored right in the middle of the April Point float plane landing field. Aboard are the first Saturday morning group of commuting-from-the-city businessmen. These are men who have left their wives and families, or spousal equivalents, up here on their boats that have been tied up to the dock at a dollar a foot a night for the week while they have been pursuing the money to pay for all of it, in a far-off city somewhere.

The people we are scheduled to meet here are easing up to the dock in their 45 foot Bayliner. An hour later, they are tied up, fendered off, and plugged into electricity, water and telephone lines. I eased towards the dock wishing that Lee Iacocca had made air bags for boat fronts, and finally manage to tie up behind them.

Laurie is off the boat as soon as we are tied up so she can have her morning shower, and I begin to stow the convertible top for another day of great sunshine. I am very used to the snide remarks of the dock walkers with their cups of coffee with their yacht name on the side and a finger or two of brandy in the bottom.

"You came all the way up here from where? In that little thing?"

"Where's your yacht?"

"My tender's bigger than that."

Mindful of the lack of monthly payments on our 20 foot yacht, remarks like these always go unanswered. People are wandering by to do whatever they do on the docks in the early morning. Most of them are mentally doing their morning wandering, security blanket reaffirmation of,

"My boat is not only longer than yours, but cleaner than yours."

By the time Laurie is through with her $1.50 shower, I have the Coleman stove hissing, the teapot on, the frying pan warming up, and the Coleman oven heating up on our second single burner stove. I hear more snide remarks from more people as they wander the docks with their perfectly matching yachting clothes with the name of their yacht embroidered on everything they are wearing. Probably on their underwear, too.

Now it is my turn for my shower at the marina office and so Laurie starts what she is a master at, Camp (or Boat) Cooking.

Fifteen minutes later when I return, there are eight people sitting on the dock around our boat, chatting and watching Laurie create toasted English Muffins, topped with poached eggs and melted cheese and half a fresh crab on top of each egg.

Smiling smugly, we sit down on the dock and devour a meal fit for a millionaire at the April Point Marina, as perfect a dock to sit on and eat breakfast as there is in the world.

One of the people standing around that we offered hot tea to while they watched us devour our great breakfast whispered, "On a boat our size, everything has to be perfect, shiny bright, swept, hosed or polished...you, with all your clutter, I know are having more fun than we are on our 94 footer."

As I attack my breakfast on the dock at April Point, I know he is right.

"You came clear up here, in that?"

PORTUGUESE MAN O' WAR

When the Windsurfer was invented 25 years ago, their sales pitch was "The Wind is Free."

That was then. This is now. A top of the line sailboard costs about $1,500. Mast, boom, and sail are another $800 or $900 and you need six or seven sails of different sizes. Then if you really get hooked on the sport, you have to buy a place at The Gorge or Maui to store your stuff when you are skiing.

You can drive your van to the Gorge. Maui is a $500 round-trip airplane ticket each time you want to use the Free Wind. You can go to your favorite spot and spend your entire vacation waiting for the wind to blow. It would be the same as if you came to a ski resort and hoped that there would be snow some of the time that you were there.

There can be giant waves, 40 mph winds, coral cuts, and things that lurk beneath the sea that sting and bite.

But the wind is free and the water is a warm, tropical, 78 degrees.

Right now the wind is blowing about 25 mph, which puts it in the four square meter sail range.

I'm windsurfing off of Sugar Cove, about a half mile, Paia-side of Sprecklesville, Maui.

Lucky? You bet.

I'm lucky because there are very few windsurfers this side of Sprecklesville and because there is a reef to ride the small swell that has bent around the island from the south. Which is just great because I'm in the learning phase of this adventure.

The North wind has been blowing steadily for the last three days and I have finally completed more than one jibe in a row, two linked jibes. I'm dedicated to the long and frustrating mastery of this, "the wind is free", sport.

I have been sailing for about three hours and have managed to crash on 62 jibes. But I have managed to complete nine.

When you are as bad a windsurfer as I am, you keep score.

"O.K. Warren. Talk your way through it."

"Depress the lee rail to start your turn as you bear off on the face of that big chop. No stupid don't step back like you did on your surfboard for all of those years. Pull the mast towards your chest just like those hotshots you watch in those "how to" videos."

Splat! Crash #63!

As I begin to get my gear sorted out, a searing pain hits my left shoulder, then screams down across my chest, the front of my thigh, and now my ankle and foot feel as though they have been dipped in scalding hot grease.

I have been stung by a Portuguese Man 'O War!

The pain takes my breath away, as I realize I am about a mile and a half out in the ocean. I know I have to go underwater to push the board under the boom, do a water start, and get to first aid on the beach as fast as the wind will drive me.

I know I'm in real trouble as I sheet in and look down and see the long tentacles of the Man O' War stuck to my chest, down my leg, and across my foot.

"Don't try to rub them off; you will only squeeze the poison out of 'em."

The poison now begins to really get into my system and my heartbeat and respiration begin to kick into a real scary high rate of speed. I have to start talking out loud to myself...real loud.

"No one I have ever known has died from one of these stings."

But then some people that I don't know have.

"It's OK."

My heart seems like it is going at about 165 beats per minute and my breath is coming in shallow gasps. The beach is getting closer. Don't get caught in the wind shadow. Drive hard.

Luck is on my side...

I stagger up on the beach and start hollering for help.

"I've been stung."

"Get me something, 'cuz I really hurt, and I'm scared."

Antidotes? There are three good ones for a Man O' War sting. Household ammonia is the best. Meat tenderizer mixed with a little vinegar or pineapple juice is next on the list. If you don't have access to either of these, you better find a few of your friends who will tinkle on your stings. They should be very good friends. The ammonia in their urine neutralizes the poison of the Man O' War and takes the sting out of your body.

I managed to locate someone with some ammonia, rather than a few people with full bladders. Within a couple of hours, most of the stinging pain was gone.

The last time I had been stung by a Man O' War was in 1944, when I was in the Navy and was bodysurfing in Florida. That was 44 years ago when I was only 20 years old, so I figure the odds would be that I would be about 108 years old the next time I got stung.

The next day the wind was a little lighter, and for the first time in my windsurfing career, I had exactly the right size sail to match the wind, 4.5 square meters.

I manage four jibes in a row. With each one of them my confidence grew. "Hey, this isn't so hard after all."

I was two miles outside, where the big ocean swells add to the height of the chop and was talking myself through my fifth jibe in a row when...Splat!

I'm getting my mast, boom, and board back together when that same searing pain hits me in the left shoulder and again shoots down across my chest. I scream in astonishment and gasp for air.

As I did, the head of the Portuguese Man O' War goes in my mouth.

As I spit it out, an excruciating fire scorches the roof of my mouth, under my tongue, all over my gums. My heart is racing faster than I had ever felt it in my life, only this time I'm two miles off shore.

My brain races as I gather my gear for the water start and head for shore.

How am I going to put ammonia in my mouth to neutralize the poison?

Will I need a ride to the hospital?

Can I function long enough to get to shore with such rapid and shallow breathing?

Will the wind shadow be there?

Will I have to swim the last 100 yards?

Will ammonia be available?

What does meat tenderizer taste like?

How can I put this stuff in my mouth and not swallow it?

Keep talking to yourself Warren....

So far, I am still able to think. The water's still warm. My gear is intact and I'm gliding to the beach. No wind shadow.

Okay, drag the gear up the beach...that's far enough. Now walk, don't run, up the steps.

Suddenly, I realize my wife is shouting at me,

"Quit screaming at me. I'm only two feet away."

A hundred feet away is the condo where I borrowed the ammonia just yesterday. Fortunately, someone is there and as they scramble for the meat tenderizer, I realize I have the ammonia bottle to my lips and am swilling ammonia around in my mouth.

Someone hollers, "For heaven's sakes, Warren, don't swallow that stuff."

I slowly sink to the ground, too weak and scared to stand any longer. My heart is beating off the scale. Respiration too rapid and shallow to get much oxygen.

I'm babbling and trying to explain to my wife and the others, "I almost swallowed the head of a Man O' War." Somewhere in the distance I hear someone say " call 911...."

Everyone at 911 was busy handling the survivors of the Aloha Airlines convertible flight that had just somehow managed to land safely at the nearby Kahalui airport without its roof. But someone at 911 does say, "There are antidotes for Portuguese Man O' War stings. Ammonia, meat tenderizer, or some friends who will tinkle on your stings...."

Not in my mouth!.

The ammonia was slowly beginning to work in my mouth. My panic was starting to subside, and about ten hours later, around midnight, I'm well enough to drive down to Kahalui and have a gigantic pineapple milkshake.

On the way home, I stopped at a Seven-Eleven and bought my own personal supply of ammonia and meat tenderizer.

With luck, I will be 152 years old before I have to use them again.

"The wind is free and the water is 78 degrees."

SO YOU WANT TO GO TO COLLEGE?

The other day I was waiting in my doctor's office, thumbing through a three-year-old copy of National Geographics and a 1987 copy of Reader's Digest. (He always makes me wait a long time.) When I discovered the latest brochure of the many classes being offered at the local community college, I settled down to read something current. This is a State college that is paid for with some of my tax dollars and so I was surprised at the variety of subjects they were teaching, subjects for which anyone could get a student loan in order to take any of them.

They had none of the classes that I would normally associate with a college. The offered no engineering, no pre-law, no pre-med, no biology, no foreign languages, not even Spanish so you could understand the local workers.

COURSES AVAILABLE AT MOUNTAIN COLLEGE
SUMMER QUARTER

BACKPACKING FOR THE BEGINNER
What kind of a pack to buy, where to hike and how far. How to tell when you are tired. How to avoid meeting someone who is a backpacker, if you aren't. What kind of rain gear to purchase when you hate to walk in the rain. Preparing dehydrated foods when you are dehydrated. How

to sleep in a tent without sliding out the end of it. How to buy hiking boots for under $250.

SELF DEFENSE FOR THE DEFENSELESS

The pros and cons of Karate vs. Mace. How to avoid the man you don't want to meet without him knowing it. How to meet the man who is trying to avoid you. Large handguns for small purses. Which kind of bullets to buy. Where to go for the quickest and most effective target practice.

TELESCOPE MAKING FOR THE AMATEUR

How to analyze the cost of the various component parts of your telescope. The reliability of PVC vs. Iron pipe. How to suspend a mirror. How to grind your own mirror for the least aberration. How far out of town to go so the night sky is dark enough to use your project when you finish it. Should you move to a colder, darker town so you can see the stars?

BASIC ROCK CLIMBING WITH AN EXPLORATORY TRIP INTO THE MINDS OF MEN AND WOMEN WHO DO

Care and coiling of climbing ropes. How to take care of your pitons so they will take care of you. How to climb without sweating. The subtle art of chalking your hands so you will look like a climber. How to tell the difference between granite, shale, and tundra. How to sleep on rocks and like it.

LOW COST, LOW CALORIE, MEAL PREPARATION

Correct ratios of hamburger helper to a variety of ingredients. Gourmet meals for pennies. How to pinch stuff from your parent's refrigerator and not get caught.

WINE MAKING FOR THE AMATEUR

What kind of grapes to buy. How and where to hide your crocks so the neighbors won't smell them. How to crush with your feet instead of a commercial press. Bottle vs. carton storage? Corks vs. caps? How to tell when your wine is drinkable. How to explain your hobby to your mother-in-law.

HOW TO LIVE WITH MANY ROOMMATES

Should your name be on the lease? How to handle telephone bills. How to decide whose name is on the gas and electricity. At what point of consumption is recycling beer cans economically viable? How to deal with your landlord when he finds too many mattresses in your apartment. Bathroom cleanup and whose trash was it. How to sort out parking privileges. Where and how to store out of season gear, including, kayaks, rock climbing, mountain bikes, skis, fishing tackle, golf clubs, tennis rackets, lawn mowers, snowplows, weed eaters, and windsurfers.

MOTOR HOME LIVING FOR THE AMATEUR

How to choose one. How to pay for one. Where to park one. How fast to drive one. How to set up a TV dish in less than two hours. Microwave cookery for the unsuccessful fisherman. How to create exciting bologna sandwiches while she is driving. Stowing dishes for mountain driving. Small hobbies for small spaces.

BASIC BICYCLE REPAIR FOR THE BEGINNER

Seat adjustment. Gear shifting when it won't shift. Tire changing and tube repair. Gear shift adjustments and how to swear in foreign languages. Care and selection of handlebars to match your basic body shape. What color bike to buy and why. Accessory selection: Spandex pants, foam helmets vs fiberglass, proper gloves. What kind of water bottles to buy and what kind of liquid to carry in them. How much to eat and drink per mile. Paniers vs rucksacks. Mountain bikes vs. road bikes.

HOW TO SURVIVE THE MUD SEASON

How to spend the evenings in the only restaurant in town that stays open. Care and feeding of your Briggs and Stratton engine. How grass clippings dry out engines. Weed Wackers for the wacky. What kind of goggles to wear. Where and how to find someone to do the chores around the house while you're fishing. How much to pay them. Per Job? Per hour? Basic household Spanish.

PROFITABLE LIQUIDATION OF FREE SKI EQUIPMENT

Where to advertise and sell what you got free last winter. How to price it. How to display it. Trade it in for what? Should you wait until fall to sell it? Ski swaps and what percentage they take off of the top. Garage sales for the goofy. How to make your worn out equipment look new.

AUTOMOBILE REPAIR FOR THE KLUTZ

How to make that nine-year-old car last another 60 days. Nine hundred and ninety-nine things you can fix with duct tape. Replacement of studded tires by people who aren't studs. Carburetor adjustment for new arrivals. Bondo, the miracle material, and how to fill up rust rot. Windshield crack repairs for the casual. Is there a new or used car in your future? What models to look for and where to shop. How to size up a car salesman by his shoes, his double knit suit, or his hairdo.

HOW TO BUILD FURNITURE
FROM NATURAL MATERIALS

Locating the just right tree limbs. Rocks can be comfortable. Basic upholstering with sheepskin. All about antlers, what kinds, sizes, and shapes.

BAGGAGE HANDLING
FOR BEGINNING TRAVELERS

Soft luggage, hard luggage, borrowed luggage? What kind to buy. New, second-hand; where to get each of them. Two big suitcases vs. six small suitcases. Wheeled luggage and what kind of wheels. What to do when your luggage doesn't arrive.

THERE'S A CAREER IN FRY COOKING

How to cook eggs so they are barely edible. Pancakes for wheels. Hamburgers with high fat content. How to make a fashion statement with a cooking hat. How to wipe your hands on your apron and still look clean. High cholesterol hamburgers. How to serve warm salads with a smile.

I was deeply involved in reading,

HOW TO CONVERT YOUR GARAGE INTO
AN INCOME-PRODUCING APARTMENT,

when the nurse finally admitted me into an examintation room where I could wait another hour for the doctor. There, I discovered the magazines that were too old for the waiting room.

"Say's she's gettin' her legs in shape for skiing."

HOW TO GET IN SHAPE FOR SKIING

Before you ever get to a ski hill, there are a number of things you have to do, in addition to getting a bank loan, to get to the ski hill.

Hundreds of books, video tapes, and magazine articles have been created about getting that flabby body of yours in shape so it can be covered up with baggy ski clothes. Jane Fonda has made millions with her tapes, and health food stores abound just so people can diet their way to a firm body.

I have skied for most of my life and a few years ago I recall doing a push-up, but I got carpet lint on my T-shirt so I gave that up. I even bought some vitamins once, but their curative powers are still locked in a bottle somewhere in my garage, along with some other souvenirs of my sporadic overindulgence in the pursuit of health.

Here are a few things to do to get in shape to ski, as well as to get in shape to get to where the skiing is.

HOW TO GET IN SHAPE FOR THAT
INTERNATIONAL SKI RESORT THAT IS
JUST A SHORT CHARTER FLIGHT AWAY

Buy a 24 inch television set, remove the set from the box, and hook it up. Place the cardboard box in the middle of the living room floor in front of the TV set. For the next month, climb into the box each evening after a hard day at the factory or at the office. Have a couple of your favorite things to eat, drink, and read alongside the box. Make sure the coffee is cold, the cold drinks are warm, and the magazines are at least a year old and all of the coupons have been torn out of them.

After your legs go to sleep curled up in the TV box, have your spousal equivalent serve you a cold, five-day-old, plastic dinner. Make sure the knives and forks are from a Barbie Doll kitchen. After you spill the coffee in your lap, watch three and a half hours of network TV rejects. No remote channel changers allowed and make sure you watch it without sound because earphones are $4 extra because this is a budget flight.

As your body falls asleep almost up to your armpits, pretend the fasten seat belt sign is on due to turbulence, and all of the bathrooms are occupied. When you can handle five and a half hours in the carton, you are ready to buy your discount ticket eleven months in advance to MT. Whatchamacallit.

THE THIGH BURNER TO AVOID THIGH BURN

This is the most important exercise in the world to do. Start doing it right now while you are reading this article:

Stand with your back against the wall, move both feet about 10 inches away from the wall as you slide your back down the wall.

Do this until your thighs are almost parallel to the floor, knees a little bit lower than your thighs, and your lower legs are parallel to the wall. Sort of like sitting in a chair.

Do this for as long as you can and each day, add ten seconds to your time. Now, if you are still sitting there with your back against the wall while you read this entire article, you are already in good shape. (When you can do this for five minutes, you are ready for a world cup race.)

AEROBICS GETS YOU IN SHAPE TO DO AEROBICS

Even though our forefathers said, "All men are created equal," we know that is a myth because we know that women are different, and I thank our forefathers for that difference.

I pose a question.

If every man, woman and child in an aerobics class in America loses a pound a day, where does all that flab go? You can't bottle it, you can't package it, and you can't sell it. Maybe it is the major cause of smog. Let's do a study! Nationwide, tens of thousands of tons of flab can be found at any one time jiggling to the beat of "The Grateful Dead," which is what most of the jigglers wished they were. Dead, that is.

GETTING IN SHAPE FOR APRES SKI OR NON-TOUCH DANCING

At home, do 3,000 deep knee bends in one hour in your quilted parka. Do this with the furnace turned up; when you can do them without sweating, you are ready to go apres ski dancing. Do it to the beat of the music and you will find that the best part of all of this gyrating, jumping, and grooving is that it shakes out all of the wrinkles in your long underwear.

BAGGAGE CARRYING EXERCISES

Fill up your two largest suitcases with vitamin-enriched tap water. Put one suitcase under each arm; then put your filled-up ski bag in one hand and your boot bag in the other. Now jog five laps back and forth to the closest Seven-Eleven store

SKIING AT HIGH ALTITUDE WITHOUT GASPING

Since the greenhouse effect is eliminating the sea level ski resorts, this is a must in your future. Since you do most of your jogging at sea level, "the paper bag over your head method" is sometimes used. (Please do not use a plastic bag.) However, this is not recommended without a jogging companion to be there to call the ambulance when you pass out.

Depending on your height, weight, and _stupidity,_ if you do this, punch a random number of paper punch holes in the bag. Place it over your head and draw it tight around your throat. Now you're ready to start your morning four mile jog. This lets you breathe a lot less air at sea level and you will sweat a lot sooner. YOU MUST USE EXTREME CAUTION WHEN YOU ARE DOING THIS EXERCISE. Always have someone with you because you will look like you have just held up a bank and are escaping with a bag over your head. This is liable to lead to your arrest.

IMPORTANT NOTE: If you run too far or too fast doing this, you will wind up with a blue face and you will be dead.

If you have read this entire article with your back against the wall, your thighs parallel to the floor, and your lower legs parallel to the wall in the artificial chair position, you can easily ski 1,000 vertical feet without resting. If you ski in Argentiere, France, you will only have to stop eight or ten times on the way down. If you ski in Wisconsin or Illinois, that 1,000 vertical feet may be as many as seven runs and this entire chapter is academic.

"Nice try George!"

DOWNHILL RACE DAY

It was a clear, cold, spring day in 1935, at the summit of the Weissflugipfel in Davos, Switzerland. Located at almost 3,000 meters above sea level, it was so clear that it seemed as though you could see clear around the world. The 43 ski racers who were going to put their life on the line for the 12 kilometer downhill race to the village of Kublis had prepared the course as best they could.

Sidestepping the almost seven miles downhill had taken days and days of preparation for the four or five racers who could spare the time from their many chores around their individual farms.

This would be the toughest downhill race ever held. The racecourse had no control gates of any kind. The courage of each individual racer was the only control necessary. Just a start and a finish line, that's all. Any route a racer wanted to take was entirely up to the individual with the racing bib on his or her back. With enough courage and ability, a racer could take all of the shortcuts he could find. He could dive through farms, rocket down icy hay sled paths, get airborne across switchbacks, and, if the snow was deep enough the day of the race, ski right over fences.

One of the better racers was overheard talking to Otto and Gertrude about removing part of their fence on the day of the race, so his line from top to bottom could be even shorter and, thus, faster.

An Italian racer was seen with a shovel, building a small pair of jumps so he could clear the wooden fences on each side of Herman's small plot of land and avoid the long way around it.

During training, the farmers became aware of the danger of a hurtling body colliding with a cow, some sheep, or even a goat. Even the chickens began to get a little skitterish as the racers practiced their innumerable shortcuts through the farmyards at the unheard of speed of over 25 mph in some sections of the route. I can't call it a racecourse because almost every racer had a different route.

It was now countdown time to the start of the race and the curious and the macabre had queued up early to ride the new-fangled Parsenn Bahn cable railway up to watch the anticipated carnage of this newly invented sport of downhill racing.

The forerunner shoved off, accompanied by encouragement from the several hundred spectators shouting in half a dozen different languages. He had a large, Swiss cowbell tied around his neck and it was clanging loudly so it could warn anyone or anything in his path to get out of the way and to be sure to tie up their farm animals.

Not one of the best skiers in the group, Wolfgang fell innumerable times on his 12 kilometer downhill journey, and finally arrived in Kublis some 34 minutes later, sweaty, and completely exhausted.

Upon his arrival, the race officials waved their special flag at the telegraph operator at the nearby railroad station to telephone to Davos Dorf, to telephone to the Weissflujoch Station at the top of the Parsenn Bahn, to raise their special flag so the race officials at the top of the racecourse would know the course was clear and now ready for the racers.

Most of the racers had no metal edges on their skis. They were a very recent invention and many of them had not even seen them before. Others considered metal edges much too dangerous to have so close to their body in the event of a fall.

One by one, the racers shoved off and, some 29 minutes later, the first one, wearing bib #3, lurched through the finish line.

Dirty and disheveled, his racing bib torn almost off his body, he reported later that deaf old Friedl had forgotten about the race and walked his cows home after their morning watering. Most of them had left droppings in the middle of his route for about 150 meters.

Racer #3 had not yet figured out what was the best kind of wax for a mixture of spring snow and cow manure.

However, racer #3 set the time to beat, a new course record, an elapsed time of 28 minutes, 11 seconds. Forget the fact that he smelled like a cow barn that hadn't been shoveled out in four months.

He always smelled that way, anyway.

One by one, the racers struggled and straggled in with their various tales of near death at ski racing speeds never before thought possible, ranging as high as 50 kilometers per hour in some places.

Herbert, finishing with a broken nose and blood all over his face, reported that his shortcut through Otto's barnyard was suddenly blocked by a string of cows on their way out to the watering trough. Without edges on his skis, he was unable to turn on the ice in the shade of the barn, and at the last second he lay down on the back of his skis and slid right under old Gretel. Or so he thought. Otto, Gretel's owner, later complained to the race officials that old Gretel had been udderly destroyed by some dumpkopf skier.

As the racers straggled in one by one, their times began to drop, until bib #19 came in under 25 minutes, and the crowd of 40 or 50 spectators and officials near the railroad station went berserk.

Mueller, who built the two jumps to get through the farmyards, missed his first jump. He didn't have any edges and when he went into a snowplow to slow down, he didn't. Instead, he did a forward 360, ricochetted off the village watering trough, scattered a herd of goats in all directions, and somehow made it to the finish line with only one ski pole and wearing only a ski and a half.

Then a young Swiss racer came hurtling out of the trees from a completely different direction, heading for the finish line with a racing number completely out of sequence. Either he had started at the wrong time or he had passed 11 or 12 racers on the way down.

His was the fastest time that day by almost six minutes.

Walter Prager, who would later become the ski coach at Dartmouth College, was the man who set the record for The Parsenn Derby Downhill that stood for over a decade.

His secret?

The right wax, skiing skill as good as anyone else on the hill that day, and his own secret weapon.

Remember, only a few people in the race had metal edges?

Walter was one of the racers who did.

He had spent a week studying the many different routes for the 12 kilometer course from the summit of the Weissflugipfel to the village of Kublis.

He had diagrammed all of the various routes, and two days before the race all of the variables came together. He finally realized that all of his left turns would be on ice or hard-packed snow, and all of his right turns would be on soft, corn snow.

The night before the race, Walter unscrewed all of the interlocked pieces of steel edges on the right-hand side of his skis and replaced them with brass edges that he had made himself. Walter Prager's uncle, an engineer and a skier too, had convinced Walter that brass edges would have a lower coefficient of friction in the warmer temperature range of the corn snow.

Thus, science entered the world of skiing almost sixty years ago.

"Very few of the racers had metal edges."

CAR POOLING

You like to ski and the finance company has just repo'd your Beemer because they selfishly wanted monthly payments for you to keep it. You chose wisely. You can get along without a car, but you can't get along without that weekend ski fix at OLD MT. PERFECT.

Care and selection of who you will car pool with is very important. It is a five hour drive so you can once again stand in your favorite lift line. That's a long time to be singing fraternity songs and drinking beer, especially when you don't drink and never went to college because of one of the wars.

This set of directions for car pooling will be broken down into several categories. Amongst them are: the care and selection of what kind of vehicle to ride in; what kind of people to car pool with; how to make them think you are paying your share; how to drive the easiest part of the trip; how to watch out for the police when you're in a hurry, which you always are; how much gear to show up with the first time; and how to handle emergencies, such as flat tires, and running out of gas.

The best vehicle to car pool in is a van. You can disappear into the far corners of it with your favorite pillow and your thumb and fake sleeping for at least two-thirds of the trip. To accomplish this sedentary goal, always arrive at the car pool meeting place early. That way you can get first grabs on choice of seats. Spread out your pillow, your sandwiches, and thermos of whatever you prefer to drink, before you offer to help put your skis on the roof or your soft bag in the cargo area. Make sure your gear is in the left-hand rear seat so at the food or gas stops when you are asleep, no one will crawl over you and wake you up.

The best part of the trip to drive is always the first part. Everyone is wide awake and you can do your hundred mile stretch through traffic and toll booths, and not have to handle the icy roads and the "do you know where we are?" questions in the convenience food store in the middle of the night.

About the time your eyelids sag because of a week of midnight oil at the factory, it is no longer your responsibility to pilot this fun wagon on its journey to waiting in line at the cafeteria for every meal for the next two days.

Backtracking to how much gear to bring.

The first trip, keep it to a minimum. Don't bring your downhill, slalom, giant slalom, and powder skis. Just one pair, please, until you have surveyed the group you travel with so that on future trips you can easily commandeer more space. It's O.K. to bring one soft luggage bag full of stuff. It's not important to wear a different outfit each day you are skiing. It's more important to please the owner of the van with whom you have mooched your ride.

Paying your way.

This is a delicate one. If you are smart, you will drive first and, at the first gas stop, pay the bill. If you try to divide the $34.27 cent gas bill by the number of passengers, minus the owner of the van somewhere in the middle of the night, you will be sure to come up with the wrong answer.

Chances are, you will run out of gas somewhere in the middle of the night. On any trip in a van you will need at least a half dozen tankfulls. Get yours over with first and everyone will think you are a great guy and a big spender. They don't know yet, that your soft luggage is full of a loaf of bread and peanut butter enough to make your cheapskate sandwiches for three meals a day. If you have already put in your tankfuls, you can let someone else walk to the nearest gas station, usually, at least a three day walk from where you ran out.

It has been my experience that a reasonable pair of binoculars are a must for the back seat of a van when you are in a hurry. Whoever rides in the back of the van should take turns tracking attacking police cars. You can spot a set of unlit red lights on top of an unmarked police car from 400 yards, usually in time to slow down before the radar intercept. When it is your turn to be the lookout, make sure the driver knows you will do your best, even though you have 20/81 vision and can't tell a Wal-Mart from an Amoco gas station from across the street.

Emergencies? There will be a lot of them. (When I am reincarnated, I want to come back as someone who doesn't know a screw driver from a lug wrench.) If you are called on to help handle an emergency and the man in charge asks you to get the jack from under the back seat, hand him a crescent wrench or a Philips screwdriver or some other non-related tool. That way, he will know your are inept. This will also give him a more macho position in the group (and allow you to sleep through the tire change).

What if you can't find someone with a van or you are 16 years old and your dad won't let you use his Mercedes convertible for the weekend because there is no ski rack for it?

Four on the floor and five in the bucket seats is how you will get there. This is O.K. because you are young and the gas mileage in a small Nissan is fantastic; in fact, gas station stops will be much fewer than the required number of toilet stops. There won't be enough room for all the passengers and the luggage, so make sure you ride in the front seat. The three passengers in the back seat will have to get in first so you can put the luggage in on top of them. (The luggage will all fit, but the passengers will arrive with their pants pressed sideways.)

What about a four wheel drive Suburban something or other? Be careful because this driver will have 2.3 kids, a golden retriever, and a condo that is five miles from where you are staying in Malcolm's Manor, formerly Ed's Bed's. (Ed recently sold it for 1.2 million dollars and has retired to Cabo San Lucas to windsurf.)

You have to stay awake the whole trip so you can get out when you drive by Malcolm's Manor or else mooch floor space for Friday night. You don't want to walk the five miles back to town in the rain, and all the local taxi drivers have gone to bed hours ago. If you plan in advance to manipulate this one, have an inflatable mattress and a down sleeping bag hidden in your rucksack, because hide-a-beds are the world's most uncomfortable place to spend the night. Except for an airline terminal chair that is nailed to the floor.

If you are unlucky enough to have to drive the last leg, wait until everyone is sound asleep.

Swing the steering wheel violently from side to side as you hit the brakes hard. When the vehicle comes to a skidding stop, all you have to say is, "Wow, that was a weird dream I just had. Sorry, if I woke you up." The adrenalin of the owner of the vehicle will instantly take over and he'll insist on driving, so you can go back to sleep for the rest of the trip.

What if you belong to a ski club group with a lot of trips ahead of you? Offer to bring the electric skillet and the Macaroni casserole for Saturday night. Never mind you are sneaking into a motel for two with a van full of skiers. Always ask to rent a back unit, out of sight of the office.

Cooking is easily accomplished in the bathroom with the ventilator fan running full blast. (Stay away from tuna casseroles because they smell the room up most.) Any frozen casserole will stay frozen from Friday night until thaw-out time, sometime Saturday night.

Car pooling is a wonderful way to save those monthly car payments and still keep on skiing and let you continue to buy the latest and greatest ski gear, instead of collecting car payment receipts.

Covet thy car pool car owner, for he is definitely an endangered species. He will transport you, shelter you, and educate you, so, regardless of how you feel about him personally, treat him the same way you treated your commanding officer when you were in the army. Learn to manipulate the system because you don't have to spend every weekend with him during the summer.

Everything I have passed on as wisdom for the Friday night trip to OLD MT. PERFECT definitely applies for the Sunday night return trip.

On this one, you have to listen to all of the war stories of turning skis, girls or guys met, addresses acquired, accidents that happened, and how you stayed somewhat dry while making 83 runs during the three inches of tropical rain that fell. Be sure you drive the first leg. If you drive later, repeat the "SWERVE - AND - JAM - ON -THE - BRAKES - AND - WAKE - EVERYONE - UP - ADRENALIN - PUMPER" on purpose. You will arrive back in town, rested, and ready to sign on for another weekend of CAR POOLING.

"Care and selection of who you will carpool with is very important."

NOT EVERYONE
TAKES A SKI VACATION

What if you didn't save up all of your money for that wonderful ski vacation to Agony Acres? What if you always took your vacations in the summer with your wife and 2.7 children?

You have made all of the arrangements. You have checked out all of the highways, motels, fast food stops, and toll bridges to that favorite campground of yours. You have your computerized, printed reservation for the Mt. Perfect Forest Service Camp Location Number 19, Space Number 1387-B, Tent Number 7.

You have that reservation card glued to your windshield as you grind up to the high country and finally locate Campground Number 19, Space Number 1387-B, Tent Number 7.

It is occupied, but the 315 pound lady assures you that her husband and the rest of the kids will be back before dark and they can be packed up in less than two hours.

"You don't mind, do you?"

"Let's see, dark this far north will probably be about 10:30 p.m."

No option, except to drive back down to the National Park equivalent of a Seven-Eleven. However, it is called a Fourteen-Twenty-Two here because everything is twice as expensive. They serve breakfast until nine in the morning, so you have a couple of hours to eat before they stop serving.

By early evening, the ice in your cooler has melted and the temperature inside your station wagon has climbed to about the same as it is in Death Valley in July.

Maybe if you went back to Campground Number 19, Space Number 1837-B, Tent Number 7, you could help the overweight family get packed up and out of your camping place a little sooner.

You do, and they do, and, finally, as the sun slowly sets in the west behind Mt. Perfect, you unpack the tent and try to drive the stakes into the non-decomposed granite with a lug wrench. That's because you left your hammer at home on the workbench in the basement. In the meantime, your kids have somehow sort of assembled the camp stove on the tailgate. They are spilling gasoline all over the car while they try to pour it into the small opening without the funnel that your wife left on the clothes dryer at home.

Fortunately, there is some life left in the car battery to illuminate the scene with your headlights as things start to fit together.

You glance up occasionally at the great view you are going to have, but, as you settle down around your campfire before retiring, a 53 foot motor home passes in front of your view of the silhouette of Mt. Perfect and parks ten feet away in slot Number 1387-A.

You know there is going to be trouble when the sign on the back of it says,

"We are spending our children's inheritance," and the Mrs. has blue hair and a pink french poodle in her arms that is wearing a big blue bow with sparklies that is tied onto a silver-studded collar.

Mr. Grey Haired Beer Belly is already busy pitching his camp and does it rather quickly.

He switches on the electric awning and it rolls out over part of your camping spot for tent Number 7.

The ten foot wide Astro Turf is now rolled out the entire length of the Motor Home.

The Butane Barbecue is wheeled out downwind which, of course, is upwind from you.

Seven folding, color-coordinated, aluminum chairs are opened and spread around the perimeter of the Astro Turf.

The portable bar is wheeled in between the aluminum chairs.

The generator is now switched on to power the color television so the lady with the blue hair can watch her favorite evening show, "Rush Limbaugh."

Mom emerges from the motorhome with her second double vodka martini in her shaky hand and a pair of double-knit, polyester slacks that she bought about 145 million calories ago. The leash for her poodle is just long enough so it can tinkle on your new tent.

While all of this is going on, camping spot Number 1388-A is being occupied by eight motorcyclists on a weekend with their spousal equivalents.

They are riding the latest Harley Davidson that can go 112 mph right out of the crate. Each motorcycle is a different color and the man and woman riding them have matching glitter-painted, brain buckets with microphones and earphones so they can talk to each other. They do this while they are riding through the heat of a summer afternoon at 65 mph in their black leather, skin-tight suits and killing flies with their faces.

One of the motorcycles has a matching colored trailer which contains miniature everything for camping, a one burner stove, dehydrated backpacking food, dry ice for the cola, pots and pans that nestle together so no one can get them apart with a tire iron, stuff like that.

One of the men is a cosmetic surgeon who specializes in tucks and augmentation and had to take a month off because of his conflict of interests.

Should he make things bigger or smaller? He has one of his recent patients with him during her adjustment period and she is acting as his weekend spousal equivalent.

Couple Number 2 is a "his and hers" duo who own a computer software business and are working on computerized simultaneous translation software.

Couple Number 3 is a drummer and lead singer in a rock band. She is the drummer and their brain buckets are yellow and black.

One half of the last couple is an unemployed contingency fee attorney who has just collected his 40% of a nine million dollar whiplash accident case.

He has decided to quit his job, travel for a year of so, and have his unemployment checks mailed to him.

As the sun slowly sets behind Mt. Perfect, it is comparative analysis time as the many campers walk through the campground to see who has the largest and most expensive camping rig.

And here comes Mr. and Mrs. Overweight in their matching yellow shorts and purple varicose veins. They have coordinated hats that hold a beer can over each ear and a straw that leads down to their chins.

As they pass by, she looks like a yellow cab with both doors open.

His stomach looks like he is smuggling 47 gallons of Jello in a T-shirt.

In the entire campground, there is not one single couple who will ever hike the four miles to the top of Mt. Perfect.

Would you, and miss any part of the camping scene?

"The man and woman riding them have matching, glitter painted brain buckets."

FREEDOM WAS
A TWO-WHEELED BICYCLE

I was cruising along the other day on my 18-speed mountain bike in a pair of cutoff Levis with my duct-taped brain bucket protecting me from death by asphalt, when I was passed rather rapidly by a group on a conducted bicycle tour.

To put my bicycle riding in its proper perspective, I have the only mountain bike in the neighborhood that was Zolatoned when I bought it. It was the top of the line choice at Wal-Mart for a little under $200. Eighteen speeds, foot stirrups, hand brakes, and a genuine bell that I can ring when I am trail riding. I need that bell to scare off the deer or bears who might be in the way when I am pedaling up a trail at about half the speed I would be going if I was hiking.

But back to the tour group that pedaled by me.

Every member was Spandex-clad from neck to ankle in the latest colors and designs. Looking like a Salvador Dali painting in motion, they went by me at three times the speed I was pedaling. Their crash helmets were all worn at a rakish angle and streamlined for more speed, which made my falling apart, duct-taped, foam, brain bucket look a little shabby. It is.

As I watched their respective fannies pumping rapidly away from me, each brilliantly colored, gluteus maximus moving in rhythm to the tour conductor's blistering pace, I couldn't help but think back to my first $24.95, balloon-tired bicycle and the freedom it gave me.

It was a genuine Schwinn and had to weigh at least 35 or 40 pounds. But, so what? When you are 12 years old, weigh about 80 pounds, it is 1936, and your grandmother gives it to you for your birthday, what difference does a little weight make?

The world was now mine to explore.

I rode that balloon-tired, single speed blue demon on every horse trail in nearby Griffith Park. It rested at the base of the famous Hollywood sign more than once. In those days, the Hollywood sign was a lot bigger because it said Hollywoodland. The sign had started to fall apart eight years before when the real estate developers went bankrupt, and the tens of thousands of light bulb sockets no longer lit up the evening sky above Hollywood.

My bicycle took many forms. It went through an era where I sported 14 red reflectors on the back fender. Another time, the fenders came off, and a pair of racing handlebars replaced the longhorn cattle-style bars that were the original equipment.

My newspaper route saw my $24.95 freedom vehicle take many other forms.

For awhile, it had a rack on the back with a big box for the newspapers. As I pedaled, I could reach back and grab a folded, gum-banded paper, and throw it expertly on my customer's porch without even slowing down. The box, however, kept me from riding my girlfriend to the movie on the back of the bike. So, I switched to a canvas bag that was very versatile. It had a big hole in the center for my neck and resembled a large saddlebag. I could wear it over my shoulders and, as I delivered papers out of the front of it, that side would get lighter until I started to choke. Then, I would swing the bag around and start throwing papers out of what used to be the back.

As I got older, almost 14, it was no longer politically correct to have a rack on the back of your bike, so I switched to a bent piece of 1" wide steel that fit in the center of my handlebars. All 150 copies of the daily newspaper that I had to deliver could fit there. I folded them and slipped a gum band around each paper, while I was pedaling between my customer's houses.

I never quite got riding at night working very well.

I had four or five different kinds of flashlights that attached to the handlebars. They ranged from a Boy Scout one that I taped on with black electrical tape, to a hotshot one that cost $3. It had a small generator that would flip over against the front tire so, the faster I rode, the brighter the light shone.

But I had to leave my bike outside at night, and the dew would soon short out the five cent batteries. Besides, it was a lot more fun to pretend to be a night fighter pilot careening along in total darkness.

My trips to the beach for a day of body surfing were always a laugh and a half. As I gradually acquired a pair of swim fins, built a plywood bellyboard, and found a big beach towel, the load to go surfing began to get to be almost too hard to pedal the 20 miles home after a day in the ocean.

Then it happened. My patrol leader in my Boy Scout troop showed up at a meeting on a genuine, high speed, lightweight, racing bicycle.

It had drop handlebars and a gear on each side of the back wheel. It had wing nuts on each side of the back axle so he could remove the back wheel quickly and turn it over, so he could use the other lower gear which had a different number of teeth on it. That way, he could ride downhill using the high gear. When he had to ride back uphill, he would stop and take off the rear wheel, flop it over, and ride back up with his lower gear.

His racing bike had no brakes at all. He wore a glove on his right hand so he could grab the rapidly spinning front tire just behind the front forks. Depending on how fast he wanted to stop, he would squeeze the tire just that amount.

Oh yes, that back wheel had no coasting ability whatsoever (technically it was called a stiff hub). Wherever he rode, his legs never stopped revolving and, as his gloved hand squeezed the front wheel, he would try to pedal backwards at the same time, which would theoretically slow down the back wheel as well.

One of my nicer evening rides on my blue Schwinn with the racing handlebars was to the Polar Palace to go ice skating on Friday nights. I would hang my speed skates over the handlebars and start out about an hour before the rink opened. I must have looked weird on a rainy Saturday afternoon on a blue, balloon tire bicycle with my ice skates on the handlebars in October in southern California!

Yes, that bicycle gave me the freedom to go wherever I wanted to go whenever I wanted to go there.

I discovered and covered southern California, from Pop's Willow Lake in the northeastern end of San Fernando Valley, to Long Beach and Malibu and every mountain road in between.

Then, one evening in the spring of 1940, I had ridden my date to the local movie on the handlebars. When we came out, I discovered my bicycle had been stolen.

Crime had begun to invade southern California in 1939, and it became obvious to me that I would have to buy a lock for my next Freedom Vehicle.

"My freedom was my two wheeled bicycle, and a matinee date with my girlfriend."

OCTOPUS ISLANDS

One of the disadvantages of getting older is that you never get to sleep all night long. That's because your prostate increases in size at the same rate as your waistline, thus causing at least one or more stumbling-in-the-dark walks per night.

On a small boat this can be a major problem. Or, it can be disastrous or rewarding, depending on how sure-footed you are.

If you are wealthy enough to afford a $500 electric toilet, the macerator still sounds like a 747 engine with a blown fan. If you have an old-fashioned cheapskate, hand pumper toilet like we do on our boat, the pump makes more noise than a little league mother protesting an umpire's call against her kid. Its wheezing screams with each stroke will wake up everyone on every boat within a mile and a half.

My solution is to try to silently climb out of our forward (and only) berth. Before I have walked five feet, I have scuffed my shins on the cold box, slid on a wet bathing suit that was right where I left it, banged my head on the closed hatch trying to get topside, and somehow done all of this without screaming in pain and waking my wife, Laurie, or anyone else, within or beyond the three mile limit.

The agony of negotiating this 15 foot obstacle course is replaced by the ecstasy of a starlit world that, when you see it, you can't believe it.

The Milky Way, The Big Dipper, Casioppia, Castor and Pollux, and the Twins; all of them and a million others are visible at the same time.

Following the curve of the Milky Way down to the horizon, I discovered the water is so still and so black that the Big Dipper is clearly visible, reflected in its glassy surface.

If I was a religious man, I would think it was blasphemous to tinkle into the cup formed by The Big Dipper.

Not being religious, I tinkled, and ten billion, zillion plankton lit up as though some unseen light switch had been turned on. It then became a contest between emptying my bladder and filling up The Big Dipper until its cup runneth over.

For the first time in my declining years, I didn't mind having a mild prostate problem. Without it, I would have slept through the night and missed "the whole, phenomenal, never before witnessed in my life, experience".

Now, in the starlight, the guaranteed-for-life, luminous dial on my watch says it is three hours until sunrise. Up here it gets light early. Days don't come up with a bang like they do farther south. If you have thin eyelids like I do, you're awake by 5:00a.m. That is, unless you cover the ports with blankets so you can fool your low I.Q. eyelids into letting you sleep an extra hour or so.

About 6:15, I am awakened by voices and wonder why anyone would anchor so close. The bay is a couple of miles long and a mile wide, with only one other boat to be seen when we went to bed last night.

When I finally went topside, no other boat was to be seen anywhere. But I could still hear the voices.

"Tank seven is all done, but two and three need some more feed. I'll have to leave early to go to Campbell River to get supplies. I have to be back by tomorrow morning."

The voices are coming from a fish farm a mile and a half away. They are talking in a normal tone of voice, but the air is so clear and quiet in this part of the world that they sound as though they are within 50 feet of our boat.

After breakfast, the tide is just right for a ride to the beach in our sometimes-inflated shore boat called "Old Leaky." It has a one-quarter horsepower motor and a gas tank that holds eleven ounces. Laurie is so good at finding good clam digging beaches that, unless she finds a place that yields ten or more clams with each turn of the fork, she looks somewhere else. In half an hour we settle for about a dozen gallons. Then we have to wash them four or five times to get most of the silt out, and then sort them, some for steaming, some for frying, some for chowder, and the rest for the party when we meet up with some fishing friends in Sullivan Bay, day after tomorrow.

With Old Leaky loaded to the plimsol mark with our easily gotten loot, we now have to drag it for what seems like, 10,000 miles across a slimy, grassy, boot-sucking-off, low tide bay. While we were food gathering, the 10 foot tide had been rapidly going out of the bay that has less slope to its bottom than a kitchen counter. After putting our boots back on for the fifteenth time, there is finally enough water under Old

Leaky to float everything. But not enough, of course, for the engine to be lowered.

I always bring my oars along because, six times out of nine, I have to row back from wherever the motor has taken us, before it dies because of lack of gasoline in its miniature tank.

With Laurie mumbling encouragement and pointing me towards the boat anchored offshore, I rowed and rowed and rowed. Finally, after about 200 yards, it looked like we could lower the engine and fire it up.

I lowered it into the ancient, mud and sandy bottom that covered the prop and oozed about a third of the way up the shaft. Holding the outboard on a 45 degree angle, I finally yanked it into life and it instantly threw sand and seaweed astern like a jet boat roaring across Sydney Harbor. With the prop gripping mud instead of water, it drove most of the boat out from under Laurie, who was in the bow. She fell on top of me and I fell back on top of the engine and it, of course, slid down deeper into the mud. But, with Japanese engineering genius on display, it wormed its way through the muck until it had enough water to operate in.

I had to wait for Laurie to climb off my inert body so I could do a class five push-up off the engine and set a wobbly course for the boat.

We cruised slowly through about 200 million, give or take nineteen, iridescent jellyfish. They look more like flying saucers than flying saucers, as they pulse up from the now deeper water. When they get to the surface, they make a slight clicking sound, then turn upside down, and pulse back down in their lifelong search for whatever they are searching for.

Food probably.

Back on the boat, now, for the final sorting of the clams by size and then dropping them down into net bags. Once that is done, we hang the bags off the swim step where they can spit out whatever dirt and gunk they have in their systems. Finally, we stow the bags in the water-filled bait tank and start getting the boat ready for our journey to the next anchorage.

<u>Which</u> anchorage is a decision we never make until sometime late in the afternoon. This is easy when there are more anchorages in British Columbia than words in a dictionary.

"With the prop gripping mud instead of water, it drove the boat right out from under us."

REALITY IN SKI ADVERTISING

What is reality? Is it that incredible backlit powder snow shot on the January cover of your favorite ski publication? Is it that triple back flip that you see Steve Stunning do on that television commercial? Can reality possibly be that wonderful four wheel drive, five-on-the-floor, $6,000 rebate station wagon hauling skiers to the top of the mountain? Is reality the words the ski resorts use to describe their better-than-perfect ski resort? Words such as:

WALKING DISTANCE TO THE LIFT

Translated, this means: A 15 minute walk to a bus that comes by every half hour that always leaves one minute before you get there. A bus that will give you a cold, bumpy, 27 minute ride to the chairlift. A bus that is really a modified truck that they use to haul hogs in the summer.

HOT WATER SWIMMING POOL
ADJACENT TO THE LODGE

Reality will reveal a jacuzzi large enough for a Cocker Spaniel to swim laps in. But, unless you get into the hot water within 30 minutes of when they take the cover off, there isn't any hot water.

MODEST PRICES IN OUR DELUXE
MOUNTAINTOP RESTAURANT

*"Okay everybody. Fasten your seat belts and
we'll be at the lift within half an hour."*

Be sure to bring your own tuna fish sandwiches, because at the Summit House they cost $6 each. A cup of coffee is $2.35. A $7.25 hamburger will reveal where they filmed that very famous television commercial, "WHERE'S THE BEEF?"

AIRPORT NEARBY

This means that the bus that takes you from the airport to the resort has a bathroom in it. That's because it stops at all 19 towns en route to deliver the mail, pick up the milk, and drop off parcels. You're in luck as it is driven by a recent Russian Immigrant who spent the last five years driving a dump truck at a copper mine in Siberia because he is used to snowy, icy roads.

ALL WEATHER HIGHWAY

Reality will show that, when it snows, our highly skilled staff of skid chain installers will be happy to put your chains on your car for only $20 per car. This is the same happy staff that puts out the skid chain control sign as soon as the snow gets as deep as a quarter of an inch.

SPORTS CENTER

In reality, this torture center was designed to be used when the snow is icy, which it usually is. That's because the head of the artificial snow-making department is a major stockholder in the sports center.

The Sports Center charges you $30 a day to do the same exercises you can do at your local Y.M.C.A. for only $4, and that's without driving 500 miles to do it. Thirty dollars to play at racquetball, aerobics, dancercise, weights, paddle tennis, or swimming. After your workout, there is a health food bar where you can buy a sprout salad that offers your choice of an additional seven different kinds of lettuce. And the salad is only $11.75. Towels and lockers are extra, of course.

COMFORTABLE ROOMS WITH A
FIREPLACE

When the smog alert on your mantel flashes and the alarm goes off, you only have five minutes to douse your cozy little fire. If you don't put out your fire within the allotted time period you will automatically be billed an extra $200, which is exactly twice what the pollution control officer will fine the condo owners when they see the smoke still coming out of your numbered and registered chimney.

TEA DANCING

Reality means that the strobe lighting will make your sunburned eyes feel better because it is only bright half of the time. The music is so loud that talking below the decibels of a Denver Broncos touchdown shout is out of the question. There is little employee housing available, so the only waitress who can afford to live here is a trust fund daughter and she has to serve so many tables that "whatever it was on the rocks" you ordered is "whatever it is in warm water" by the time she gets it to you.

That very valuable fur coat you borrowed from your sister who married the right doctor or lawyer is too valuable to check, so it is resting in your lap. Your legs are all sweaty while you watch everyone jumping up and down five feet away from each other. This is your first Apres Ski experience.

Probably your last too.

You are single, so you wait to be asked to dance while you are sitting in a chair three inches off the floor swaddled in that fur coat and sprawled out with your knees up around your chin, making you feel like your first teenage visit to the gynecologist.

TRAIL MAPS

In Reality, trail maps are something someone spent a lot of money on to have wavy lines drawn all over a painting of AGONY ACRES. The artwork is designed to make the mountain look as though you are in a helicopter above the parking lot. Once the art work is done, it is reduced to the size of a postage stamp so the resort can sell advertising around the edges and pay for the artist's trip to Europe to go skiing.

From the parking lot, it's "Let's see, old White Knuckler is to the left from the top."

"Right?"

At the top of the hill, reality makes you turn the map upside down. Old White Knuckler is now to the right. Reality is that all of the trail names are now upside down and impossible to read. "DEAD MAN'S DIVE" becomes "EVID S'NAM DAED." Your new lady friend bets you a steak dinner "EVID S'NAM DAED" is to the left as you look down. She reads the map the right way and you read it your own macho way.

Two hours later, at the bottom of the lift you find out that you have just negotiated "NON-YAC HTAED." And you come to grips with the fact that she was right, and you were being macho and not listening, and ski resort maps are only to be read in the parking lot, not at the top of the mountain.

Reality in ski resort advertising means there is great imagination in ski resort advertising!

BUNGEE

L'Aiguille du Midi looms almost vertically above us as we glide silently through the sky almost 3,000 feet above the jagged rocks below. In the distance, Mt. Blanc rises to above 15,000 feet; its sun-splashed dome is buried over 1,000 feet deep in places by snow and icy glaciers. A plume of blowing snow stretches off to the northeast in a thin line against the dark blue morning sky. In the battered telecabin, everyone speaks in whispers, as though in a church.

We are all whispering through fear that the ancient cable holding us up here won't last another trip.

I'm sandwiched in between half a dozen guys up here to attend, what must be, a garlic dealer's convention. They obviously have had less than three hours sleep since their ten hour test-tasting of garlic from around the world.

There is another group, high school kids from Munich, who have a trip voucher for the ride up and back and are trying for the world's record of high altitude rowdyism. All in all, it is a standard day in a telecabin that has somehow survived for decades, survived the buffeting wind, the scared to death tourists from Iowa, and the warning voices of the guides as they get their clients ready for the trip down the glacier. Each guide has his or her favorite death-on-the-glacier story to tell.

Standing in the window on my left is a guide who is patiently explaining in halting English to his four American customers,

"Le Mir de Glace really is a ski run over eight miles long on snow and ice that, in places, is over 1,000 feet deep."

"It's sort of safe. As long as you don't make a mistake and ski into a crevasse and die." "Lucky you have me along, because so far this winter I have only lost three customers."

"We never did find one of them. He must have dropped about 500 feet down that crevasse."

"Not to worry, though."

My rucksack full of cameras, my skis, and my tripod are resting against my legs and shoulder as I stare down, 3,000 feet to the distant rocks below through a hole in the wooden floor, worn thin by the thousands of skis, boots, and climbing shoes during the many years this lift has operated. It's the same hole I noticed last year when I was up here. Except, it is a little bigger. Maybe someday someone will fall through the floor and then they will have to fix it.

This is a ski lift that rises 10,000 vertical feet in two sections. The upper section rises a little over 5,000 vertical feet with no towers from top to bottom.

The telecabin is slowing down now for its arrival in the top terminal, its motion guided by some unseen, half-asleep engineer, down in the bowels of the machinery that brought us up here.

Stopping gently, it is quickly emptied. Now each passenger, tourist, mountain climber, garlic importer, and skier, gropes his way through the long, dark tunnel hollowed out of this solid needle of granite. I stay behind for a moment to watch the battered red telecabin, its roof covered with grease and dirt from the many sheaves it rides up and down on, drop almost vertically towards the lower terminal 5,000 feet below.

"Someday I'm going to ride up here and then ride right back down and take movies of what it feels like to take that 5,000 vertical foot drop. I could open the hatch in the roof and run the camera as the lift drops," I thought.

I groped my way through the long tunnel, across the bridge, and out the other side of the granite needle. The eight mile long glacier curves away to the left below us and disappears into a zero visibility fog bank. A rope barrier with a FERME! (closed) sign is stretched across the three flights of stairs that lead down to the snow and ice.

"It looks like I can get those shots riding down in the telecabin sooner than I expected."

Five cups of tea, two crescents and a lot of marmalade later, my four skiers and I are standing in an empty telecabin with the hatch in the roof open. I have my chance to run my camera and create the feeling of falling through space. One of my four skiers speaks French and a chair mysteriously appears for me to stand on. Now I can get my head and shoulders above the roof and get a variety of scenes.

"Are you ready?"

"Yes."

Suddenly, four sets of arms grab my legs, throw me up on the greasy roof, slam the hatch shut, and the telecabin suddenly begins to drop. I grab hold of anything I can hang onto. Riding down on the greasy roof, 5,000 feet above the rocks and ice, I feel like I am trying to hang onto the roof of an airplane coming in for a crash landing.

And I don't have a parachute.

Recently, a friend of mine came back from Chamonix and said,

"Warren, your fingerprints are still in the aluminum roof of that telecabin, 20 years later."

"But, they told me to tell you they finally put a new floor in it."

My friend had been part of the World's Record Bungee Jump that was set from this same telecabin.

The lift had been leased for two hours by a French film production company. The bungee was laid out very carefully on the floor because it had to absolutely flow out the door smoothly as the jumper fell through space. Cameramen were stationed all over Chamonix with two and three thousand mm lenses, so they could get this world's record free fall bungee jump from every angle.

By the time the telecabin had reached its highest point above the ground and stopped for the final preparation, the concerned conductor on board had tried to interrupt the plans at least half a dozen times.

Now radios crackled between the various cameramen, the director, and the jumper.

"Ready?"

"Yes" was the reply from all five cameramen.

"Jumper ready?"

"Yes."

With that, the conductor stepped in front of the jumper one more time, and said,

"Don't you think you should tie the end of the bungee to the telecabin before you jump?"

They did.

The jump went off spectacularly, as the bungee finally stretched to the end of its elasticity 2,000 feet below, where it yanked the jumper back up three or four hundred feet. Then, it took almost five minutes for him to finally stop going up and down.

Anticlimactically, the telecabin was slowly lowered until the jumper could touch the ground, where he was untied from his bungee. Elated, excited, wired, he was happy to still be alive, but the Chamonix doctors insisted on taking him to the hospital for a checkup, just in case.

Upon close examination, they discovered that he was three inches taller than before he jumped.

SKIING BUZZ WORDS

Recently, I sat next to a young lady on an airline flight who told me that she was on her first "Learn to Ski" trip. After being served the standard, miniature, airline meal, she pulled out a two-year-old magazine from the seat pocket in front of her. She couldn't understand much of the article about skiing that she was reading. So I offered my years of experience to help her learn what some of the Skiing Buzz Words really meant.

Most of them are an equal mixture of advertising agency jargon, hip and groovy MTV talk, and an editorial snow job.

Here's what the words really mean:

QUAD LIFT

A four million dollar device that floats through the air at a high rate of speed that you cling to during a windy blizzard for what seems like hours. You quite often will sit downwind from three total strangers who are smoking and haven't had a bath since they left home four days ago.

MAN-MADE SNOW

A commodity that takes vast quantities of coal to generate electricity to expensively convert water to ice on the side of a steep hill. This allows you to pay $45 a day to wait in a lift line and look at it while a college graduate who is earning $6 an hour tries to get it running again.

SKIER DAYS

The supposedly, exact number of all day lift tickets sold at any given resort during the winter. A number that is flexible so the last person to be the marketing director can always exaggerate this number.

INSURANCE

A mysterious piece of paper that allows contingency fee, ambulance chasing attorneys to write off their ski vacations while listening to the ski patrol radio channel so they can monitor accidents. This increases the cost of your lift ticket 25%.

TRAVEL AGENT

The company that will book you into the wrong room, at the wrong hotel, at the wrong end of town, at the wrong time of the year, at the wrong price, when the snow level is down to 14,000 feet.

P.R. DIRECTOR

Someone who used to sell used cars before he washed dishes last month before he joined the ski patrol and patched up the leg of the wife of the owner of Bellyache Mountain.

MERGER

When two failing ski resorts climb on the same toboggan to ride down what's left of their financial statement.

PISTEN BULLY

A $200,000 device that smooths out all of the bumps in the snow, because anyone over 35 would quit skiing if they hadn't been invented.

SNOW GUN

A very expensive device to spray small drops of water onto rocks and stumps so that they can, under a mild drop in temperature, slowly coagulate into homogeneous, frozen, icy masses the size of subcompact cars that the skiing press call moguls.

SNOW REPORT

An ambiguous, hypothesis of potential snow conditions by the creative writing of an assistant marketing person who is looking for a better paying job.

PHENOLIC SIDEWALLS

Kind of like white sidewall tires, only they are on the side of a ski instead.

CELLULAR PHONE

A group of cheaply produced microscopic things in a cheap, exotic, high tech, plastic case that someone invented so that a ski vacation away from the office is a thing of the past.

ARTIFICIAL FIBER

Something that cost about 14 million dollars in research and development so a chemical company could duplicate the feathers of a Chinese duck.

MULTI MATRIX LAMINATES

Man-made snow that is laid down over rocks, ice, and the four inches of powder snow they got in the last storm that covered the slush that came out of the snow guns when the temperature shot up to 41 degrees at 3:00a.m. this morning.

POWDER HOUNDS

A semi rare breed of dogs that spend all winter trying to track up a new powder snow-covered slope.

LIFT LINES

Something you pay up to $45 a day to stand and freeze in, unless you can pay an extra $300 a day for an instructor, so you don't have to.

"Steig's the name, skiin's my game."

ADAPTS EASILY TO ANY ENVIRONMENT

A 53-year-old ex-husband wearing a gold chain and sporting a hair transplant, who is in search of a lift riding companion, a free dinner, and lodging for the night, while he looks for his next ex-wife.

HELI SKIING

A very exotic, noisy, and scary way to become the most listened to person at all of the summer cocktail parties.

CROSS TRAINING

A religious rite performed while bathed in sweat so you will be in shape for the upcoming season's sport. Devotees never have to participate in competitive seasonal sports. They are always cross training for the upcoming season.

INLINE SKATES

A new plastic device to strap on your feet so you can get there and back faster, with all of the skin scraped off of your hands, knees, elbows, and shoulders.

VACUUM TECHNIQUE

How your room gets clean when you're skiing, if the maid shows up on time, which she won't, because today is a powder snow day.

ULTRA-SAFE

The bench to occupy in the sun at the bottom of the chairlift.

DIAGONAL KEVLAR LAMINATE

Something added to a pair of skis to substantially raise the cost of same.

SPECIAL DISCOUNT

The mystical and hypothetical discount that is subtracted from the retail price of any ski product after the normal markup has been doubled.

CERAMIC TECHNOLOGY

This is when the snow making machines produce snow that is the same texture as your pottery dishes.

SNOWMOBILE

A $7,852.00 mechanical device that will travel over ice and snow at a rapid rate and transport you from bar to bar after your driver's license has been suspended because of too many D.W.I. convictions.

SNOWCAT

See Pisten Bully

SKID CHAINS

A device that is impossible to put on your car wheels when the Highway Patrol tells you to. However, there is always a man standing at the chain control sign who will put them on for you for a couple of $20 bills.

FOUR WHEEL DRIVE

An expensive mechanical device attached to the front axle of your car that allows you to drive over mountain passes without giving the skid chain applicator a pair of $20 bills.

FREESTYLE

A method of skiing that lets you ski differently from any other ski technique (i.e. upside down). A lot of money can be made doing it, if you ski differently enough.

FREE-LANCE REPORTER

An unemployed writer whose opinion can only be bought with free lift tickets, condos, meals, transportation, or ski equipment. Most are of senior citizen status or older.

ALL AREA EXPERT

Someone who lives in his van, can forge any lift ticket ever invented, and hauls people from one ski resort to the other for gas, wine, beer, and groceries.

FULL SPECTRUM, TWIN CAM

Twins named Bob and George Cameron who run a color video company at Kissing Bridge, New York. They will video your learn-to-ski week for $125 an hour or per run, whichever comes first.

REAR ENTRY UNISEX BOOT

This is an advertising gimmick to try to satisfy the ACLU demands of equal opportunity that doesn't work for either sex.

AMERICA'S LARGEST

If it applies to anything except vertical rise of the ski lift, be careful when you make your reservations. Other things that are America's largest are the Los Angeles Freeway system, The New York City Subway, The Aswan Dam, The Grand Canyon, and Domino's Pizza.

SKIWEAR FOR PEOPLE WHO REALLY SKI

Where else would you wear it, except to ski? To a board of directors meeting? Out on your first date in Atlanta? Maybe. Obviously, to a Halloween party.

VARIABLE FRICTION CORRECTION

The salt they forgot to put on the icy bridge that you skidded into the railing on, because you wouldn't pay the skid-chain-putter-onner a pair of $20 bills.

AUTO CONTROL

Someone who wears an orange vest and makes $5.25 an hour while he tells you where to park your brand new $39,000 car with your four pair of skis and poles on the roof.

THE SPIRIT OF SKIING

Lowering lift ticket prices, moving the ski resorts closer to the city, and being able to make artificial snow when it is sunny and 40 degrees.

GO OVERLAP

When your inside ski tip overlaps your outside ski tip, you go over your lap and land on your face.

PILL RESISTANT, CHILL RESISTANT FABRIC

When you wear this one there are no drugs, no pills, no fever, and no more hot flashes.

PLASTER

A white, semi-hard substance that skiers used to wear to call attention to their accidents, before the invention of arthoscopic surgery.

TRI-FLEX-CONTROL

When you try to sneak in the head of the triple lift line, a $5 an hour, bearded, ponytailed, overweight, college graduate, lift loader will holler loud enough so everyone within a mile and a half will know that he is the lift loader and he is sending you to the back of the line.

TOTAL WRAP INDICATOR

This is when the ski patrolmen gives you a duct-taped, thumbs up while you are being transferred from his toboggan to the ambulance.

BLACK DIAMOND

Something you can safely promise your new date if she can ski one with grace and beauty.

By the time I got this far explaining what the Ski Magazine ads meant, it was time to land. Before we did, my seatmate handed me her business card. Did you know that PSIA means Professional Ski Instructors of America?

DO IT NOW!

For the last 45 years, I've had the best job in the world. I've traveled all over the world with a camera crew, skied almost every day all winter, and produced about 500 movies of the world's best ski resorts and skiers. Over the years, I have met a lot of very interesting people. For example, one day with the powder snow knee deep, the sky a deep cobalt blue, and the brilliant sunshine being etched in my brain and on the emulsion in my camera, I stopped to rest. As I was figuring out where to film next, someone skied to a stop just below me and said,

"You're Warren Miller aren't you?"

"Yes."

"I just had to tell you that my father hates you."

This seemed to be a rather unusual way to start a conversation with a stranger. Being smooth is not one of my better attributes, but I thought I spoke rather thoughtfully when I asked,

"Why?"

"Let me ride up on the lift with you and I'll tell you the whole story."

This guy had all the right moves, slouched on his ski poles with one resting under his armpit, the right amount of duct tape on his faded gloves, and the elbows of his parka a little worn. I knew right away that he was between 25 and 35 because he had the mustached, insecure look of that age group; they are looking for identity and not knowing how to get it.

Once we got through the lift line and settled down on the lift, he told me his story.

"When I was a little kid, my Dad used to take me to your personal appearance lectures with your film presentations in the Ford Auditorium in Detroit. You always showed up with the film the night before Thanksgiving and the first two or three times I went, I'd sit in my Dad's lap and scream and shout like everyone else did, I didn't know why I was screaming and shouting, but it seemed like it was the thing to do.

I remember when you showed Vail on the screen the first year it was open and you said, "Get out and discover it before everyone else does." My dad made Christmas reservations for us the next day and dragged the entire family out here.

Me, my two brothers, and my mom complained all the way from Detroit to Colorado, but dad drove nonstop in our station wagon. We had to stay clear down in Glenwood Springs and drive back and forth every day. We discovered everything you had said about it was true. I really got hooked, though, the first time dad skied down to Mid Vail with me between his legs.

From then on, it was an annual family trip for the Christmas holidays and, after about three years, we added Easter week. But, it was tough for my dad to budget the money and the time to drive.

We couldn't afford to fly because he was putting all the profits back into the big factory that he owned that made automobile radiators. One Easter week, he didn't even get to go with the family because he was having union problems and had to stay home and solve them. By that time, of course, we were all hooked on skiing. Mom did almost all of the driving on that trip; when she got sleepy, I did some of it across Iowa and eastern Colorado when we thought the police wouldn't see me, since I wasn't yet 16.

That Easter I got to be pals with the ski patrol and, when we got home, I got my first aid certificate. The next year, I started working part-time as a ski patrolman during Christmas and Easter week. By this time, I was in college but I was out in Colorado more than in college.

I managed to study enough between ski trips to get by. I got my degree three years ago and finally settled down and started to work full-time for my dad. My dad had always told me that I would someday be taking over his radiator engineering and manufacturing business. Every day at work, he would tell me how he could hardly wait to retire and turn the whole business over to me.

Then it happened.

I came back into the plant after a Christmas holiday of powder snow skiing, full moon nights with ten zillion stars shining, meeting and skiing with wonderful people, and enjoying great dinner parties. As I wandered around the factory and heard the noise of manufacturing, I thought, "Is this where I want to spend the rest of my life?"

That same day I took my Dad to lunch and said,

"Pop, I just can't do it. Jane and I are going out to Colorado and I'll be a ski patrolman for a year or two. I can work construction during the summer while I look around for some business to get into. I just don't want to spend my life running the factory. I'm sorry."

He knew arguing was useless and, with a tear in his eye, you know what my Dad said?

"If only I hadn't taken you to so many Warren Miller films, I could be moving out to Colorado instead of you. I really hate that Warren Miller! I wonder how many other peoples' lives he has messed up with those ski movies of his?"

The lift ride was almost at an end about the same time as that statement of his father's; he looked off to the east toward the Gore Range and said,

"D'ya mind if I ski down behind you?"

"And, oh yeah, Warren. I want to thank you for messing up my life."

"The next year I worked part time on the Ski Patrol during Easter."

MAGAZINE ARTICLES
I'M GLAD I NEVER WROTE

Over the years I have submitted many different magazine articles to special interest magazines, magazines such as, *Bicycle Monthly, Skiing For Fun and Profit, Turn Your Hobby Into Cash, Tax Deferments For The People Who Don't Need Them, Muscle Building Monthly,* and *Lawn and Garden Care For People Who Care.* Getting the editors to buy them is another story. I have a substantial share of rejection slips from these magazines and numerous other ones as well. In fact, I rate my articles by how many rejection slips they attract.

If you were an editor of a special interest magazine, how could you turn down some of the wonderful articles that I have created and have received rejections slips for?

How to Turn Your Attic Into a Recycling Center
How to Convert Your Fuchsia Garden into a
        Shuffleboard Court
Creative Garage Storage
Your Attic Can be an Inexpensive Sauna
Backyard Baseball, Basketball, Badminton, and
        Beer
How to Make End Tables Out of Your Beer Kegs
How to Make Your Bonsai Trees the Biggest in
        the Neighborhood
How to Color Your Asphalt Green
Station Wagon Picnics Can be Fun

Four Wheel Driving for City Folks
Creative Computer Decoration
How to Turn Your Table Lamp into a Barbecue
Real Estate Advice for the Beginner: Buy Low,
    Sell High
Hedge Pruning When You Have Nosey Neighbors
How I Turned My Backyard into a Parking Lot
Antique Collecting Without a Station Wagon.
Three Wheel Bicycle Riding for the Adult
Blackberry Bush Training
Look Alike Clothes for People who Don't
How to Raise Smog Reducing, Lawn Mowing,
    Goats
Farm Clothes Can be Beautiful
How to Make Your House Look Like a Barn
The Passion of Spring Planting and Manure
    Selection
The Interrelationship of Trees and Shade
How to Work Like a Dog and Still Dress
    Like a Trust Fund Adult
Cellular Phones Can be Interruptive
Calories Can be Contagious
Color-Coordinating Your Out-Buildings
The Care and Feeding of Your Garbage Disposal
Bird Dropping Removal for the Beginner
Endives to End All Salads
Real Chefs Don't Use Microwaves.
Antique Auto Collecting and Storage Problems
Tax Deductible Farms and You
Art Deco Dishwasher Repair
Your Kitchen Floor, Your Playground, and You
Fashion, Fun, Farms, and Fertilizer
How to Feather Your Nest...With Money
So You Want to Buy an Island...Why?
The Bold Look of Fat
Electric Fences Can be Profitable
Down to Earth Basics of Tree Felling

Band-Aids, Blisters, and Utopian Dreams
Little Known Napa Valley Gas Stations
Trophy Displaying for the Parent
Creative Bead Work Projects to do During TV
      Commercials
Postcard Messages to Evoke Envy
How to Cook Liver and Like It
Inexpensive Places to Park Your Jet Airplane
Sun Bathing, Tan Lines, and Cellulite
Boat Building in Your Hot House
What to do on Your Sun Porch in the Winter
Snow-Covered Skylights Can be Cold
Tuxedo Shine Removal
How to Build a Swimming Pool for $84.00
Hot Tubs and Cold Bodies
How to Filet Coi Fish
Gold Fish Training for the Beginner
Sunbathing in the Olympic Peninsula Rain
      Forest
How to Make a Bathroom Out of Your Darkroom
Remodeling Kitchen Closets Can be Fun
Linoleum is Always Underfoot
Is Plumbing Your Second Career?
How to Display Your Displays
Guide to Successful Potting While Potted
Weeds Can be Fun
Advanced Lawn Edging
Prune Low for High Yields
Tax Deductible Wine Making
Still Photography for the Active
Manure Spreading Made Easy
Diet Junk Food for the Obese
Organizing Your Drawers
How to Discourage Weekend Guests
How to Make Your Guest Beds Beautiful, but
      Lumpy

"IF YOU CAN'T CARRY IT, DON'T TAKE IT"

Late one evening we had to transfer trains in Switzerland with a five minute connection across nine sets of railroad tracks. There were three of us with 12 suitcases, six pair of skis, three pair of boots, and not a porter in sight. By this time in our train trip through Europe, we had developed a system. I would jump off the train as it was coming to a stop and run down the platform to where I was alongside the compartment we had occupied. When the train came to a stop, I would be there to catch everybody's luggage as they threw it out to me.

That night, my traveling companions had been into a bit too much of the sauce, and they heaved the first big suitcase out the window before they bothered to open it. Fortunately, the glass shattered cleanly. The first suitcase was the biggest, so the rest of the suitcases followed neatly through the broken window.

From that moment on, I decided to cut down on my luggage. Now, if I can't carry it all by myself in one transfer, it doesn't get taken.

How do you do that? Until 1970, they weighed your luggage when you got on a plane. Forty pounds and that included your carry-on luggage. That was it. I made more trips to Europe than I care to think about wearing my ski boots and my specially designed overcoat with the 14 inside pockets. If I packed all of my camera gear carefully, I could get that overcoat up over the 100 pound mark and not stagger too much. I walked and looked a lot like The Hunchback of Notre Dame but even lumpier.

I used to always take my tweed suit and a couple of bow ties because everyone used to dress for dinner. Two nylon wash-and-wear dress shirts was plenty. You had to wash your clothes after each wearing or you would be carrying around a 40 pound suitcase full of dirty clothes. Once your dirty clothes got ahead of you, you were in real trouble. I always took three extra pair of wool socks. That was because, during the three week ski trip, my $24 custom-made leather ski boots would stretch at least two or three pair of socks worth. My boots would also be soaking wet every night, but the hall porter would always dry them out and shine them up for me free of charge.

You just put them outside of your room, and about ten or eleven o'clock he would gather everyone's ski boots, chalk the room number on the bottom of them, put 'em in a basket, take them to the basement, shine them up, and have them back before you got up in the morning. One night before he picked them up, we walked down the hall and switched everyone's around before he chalked their room numbers on the soles. I quickly got in the habit of doing that on any snowy night. That way, I could have a few extra powder snow runs the next morning while the rest of the guests were trying to sort out their own ski boots.

Forget your electric razor. Everything was 220 volts and occasionally 440 volts. Anyway, a package or two of razor blades weighed a lot less than an electric razor and they took up a lot less room too. Plug your electric razor into the wrong socket and you were "Electro Man."

One pair of black ski pants, one dark blue or red parka, two sweaters and a pair of white turtle 'T's would round out your ski wardrobe. Underneath it all, a smart traveler would bring along a large supply of soap and one change of underwear. Washing your clothes every evening was always done between tea dancing and dinner. That 15 minutes a day doing laundry always saved carrying around that 40 pounds of dirty clothes.

And when you had four and five minute train changes, that extra weight could usually make you miss your connection.

If you can't carry it yourself, don't take it along.

To practice for this type of luggage carrying, I advise travelers to put two, one gallon jugs of water in each of their two suitcases and go jogging after dinner. Unless you can jog a mile in under nine minutes with a suitcase in each hand, you are taking too much stuff.

Then there were always your skis.

They could be carried 10,000 different ways.

All of them uncomfortable.

After-ski boots were quickly replaced with a good pair of tennis or basketball shoes. That way, you could be light and quick on your feet when your partners forgot to open the train window. What about travel arrangements? You used to stop by a travel agency and they would hand you three or four brochures, a map, an airline schedule, and that was it. They would try to book you on one of their Love Boat cruises while you made up your mind where to go skiing. The decision was usually based on the pictures of Freidl Furst and Freida Frump standing in front of a mountain restaurant somewhere, sipping wine with their white socks outside of their ski pants. This was never the resort you got booked into.

Do all of this and you won't have to learn to travel the hard way.

The way I did.

By throwing luggage through train windows in Switzerland 45 years ago.

"In my fourteen pocket overcoat I looked like
The Hunchback of Notre Dame."

STRAIT OF GEORGIA

From time to time over my lifetime of boating, both sail and power, I have thought about equipping one of my boats with RADAR. When I lived in southern California, I didn't need it. Sail 180 degrees from Marina Del Rey and you hit Catalina; sail zero on the way home and you will hit the mainland. Cruising in the Northwest you are always in sight of land, so whenever my wife and I discuss buying RADAR for our boat, it is always at the bottom of the list behind a ski trip, a new washing machine, or the need for a new printer for my word processor.

We chatted about RADAR a while ago when it was raining half an inch an hour for five hours, and the wind was blowing 30 mph out of the south. We were slogging south from Heriot Bay to Pender Harbor before crossing the Straits of Georgia. We didn't really chat about it. In fact, I tried to ignore my wife's pleading screams as we beat ourselves half to death heading into four foot seas. The waves were slamming up against an outgoing tide, so the fetch was only about the length of our 28 foot boat. The rain had reduced the visibility to less than 200 feet.

On top of that, we had lost our foul weather gear somewhere since the last rain storm, and were wearing see-through plastic jackets we had bought at the supermarket for $1.95. We covered those with garbage bags, out of which we had cut holes for our arms and head. But what really looked dumb was the zip lock bags we had fashioned for hats. (The hats worked a lot better than the jackets, I might add.)

But, that bad weather was over and after a heavy night's sleep at the dock, we awoke early to a windless, clear beautiful morning. I am standing on the sun bridge of my made-in-Florida, 28 foot, power cruiser. It is capable of 47 mph and can cruise all day long at 30 mph, except for gasoline stops every 150 miles.

Designed to sleep six, according to the advertising, it comfortably offers shelter to two consenting adults quite nicely, thank you. It can leave a lot of miles behind its transom while whistling out to the warm Florida Keys with two people in bathing suits and a small refrigerator full of libations.

I bought the boat from a bankrupt boat dealer who was located downwind from the Hanford, Washington, Atomic Energy plant and he guaranteed that the boat was not radioactive.

So far, we are both still able to get through the x-ray machines at the airports.

Soon after buying it, my wife, Laurie, and I launched our bankrupt boat smack dab into the wild weather and tidal changes of British Colombia, tidal differences that measure as much as 18 feet and currents as high as 16 knots.

Since it is a made-for-Florida boat, I always drive it in my Florida boat clothes, just like all the ads show:

Shorts and T-shirt.

This morning though, over my shorts, are two pair of sweatpants. Over my T-shirt are two sweatshirts, a ski parka, a Gore-Tex windbreaker, and a foul weather rain jacket of ripped see-through plastic. The thermometer has barely climbed above 40 degrees and it is the first time in four days that we have been able to travel comfortably. With rain measuring as much as four inches a day for the last four days, the weather finally looks good enough to try crossing the 30 miles of the Strait Of Georgia. Comox radio has reported,

"Visibility Unlimited; Sea Rippled."

Several hundred barn-sour boat owners who have been tied up three-deep at the docks, or are anchor-dragging around the bay around the clock, are trying to get underway at the same time. They have been storm-stuck for the last four days here in Pender Harbor. Meanwhile, the grass was still growing in their backyards somewhere down south, just itching to get mowed.

As we swung around the corner of the rocks that shelter the Royal Vancouver Yacht Club out-station, riding gently at anchor was an incredible powerboat that Laurie estimated to be in the 80 to 90 foot range. It is another "Miller Law of the Sea" that any yacht over 60 feet has every right to anchor anywhere the owner feels like anchoring, even if it is right in the middle of the channel, whether you like it or not. Besides, if the owner anchored his pride and joy off in a secluded cove somewhere, no one would notice it.

That yacht had everything: the right kind of dinghies hanging from the right kind of davits; the smell of fresh-baked bread coming from their automatic bread-making machine to cover the diesel fuel smell of the boat; two deckhands out wiping the rain drops off all the bright work before the owner got up; the 40 KW generator throbbing its opposition to the serenity of the wispy morning fog that still embraced parts of the harbor; down riggers, salmon poles, and fish nets at the ready on the 22 foot powerboat on the aft cabin top. Nestled just in front of the flying bridge with matching chrome-plated davits were a pair of jet skis painted to match the bright yellow hulled 86 footer. They were covered with color-coordinated canvas covers.

The owner had more invested in canvas covers than we had invested in our 28 foot Florida boat. And, yes, he also had two radars.

As we passed close abeam, I noticed some rather furious activity on the flying bridge.

Closer scrutiny revealed two chartreuse, purple, and black, Spandex-clad ladies. They also wore white-rimmed, wrap-around sunglasses. They were blonde, probably plastic-chested starlets, working out on their matching exercycle machines. Since my wife says ladies don't sweat, they glow, these bodies "glistened" in the backlit, early morning sun. No one ever told them that their aerobically tightened bodies with I.Qs. that matched their waistlines would be completely covered up most of the time in the British Columbia weather, covered up with matching, yellow foul weather gear that is big enough to cover a six foot tall, pregnant Kangaroo. As we passed the stern of this fine, canary yellow vessel, we duly noted that it was out of Marina Del Rey California.

Of course, it was named "TIT-ILLATING."

Near the entrance to Pender Harbor, I eased the throttles forward, got the boat up onto a plane, and swung southeast.

Destination, Silva Bay on Gabriola Island.

The sea was not even rippled. The ever-widening V wakes of the boats that had left earlier could be seen crossing each other as far as half a mile astern of each other.

It was going to be an easy crossing, and we would be refueling in Silva Bay in about an hour.

As the Thormanby Islands were abeam on our port side, we ran into a wall of fog that made you feel like you where scuba diving in a swimming pool full of milk. We couldn't see 50 feet.

Make that 35 feet.

So much for our 30 mph cruising capability without radar.

We backed off to about two mph and bugged each other with, "I told you we should have gotten radar for our boat instead of that new snowplow for our driveway."

Steering between 130 and 157 will get you a landfall somewhere between Nanimo and Silva Bay. At two mph, it was going to be a seven or eight hour crossing. With several hundred boats making the crossing from Pender this morning, I kept trying to reassure Laurie that we would eventually be overtaken by someone with radar and we could follow them into a port of some kind.

I secretly wondered if we weren't already on a collision course with a ferry boat out of Vancouver, or a freighter bound for Alaska, or maybe crossing between a tug and the barge it was hauling. Would we get hung up on the towing cable?

We thought we were on course when we heard the first foghorn, but we couldn't find any lighthouses on our chart whose signal corresponded with this one. It got louder and louder until the pitch of it changed as it went by on our port side. Neither of us saw the boat until it was within 25 feet of us, going about ten knots in the opposite direction. He obviously had radar. As they passed, their foghorn was replaced with a litany of four letter words accusing us of being from California and what they thought we could do with our well-founded yacht before, after, or if we ever bought our own radar.

Almost immediately, we heard another foghorn. But this one was astern of us and slowly closing. Ten agonizing minutes later, it emerged from the fog about 50 feet astern and altered course, its skipper waving "hello" as they passed. We waved back and then spent the next four agonizing hours staying between the V of the ever enlarging, bow waves of this boat. We were sure it had radar, because we could see the radar housing above his cabin.

After hours of trying to keep exactly in the center of his wake, I was beginning to get very sleepy when, suddenly, he made a sharp left turn. Assuming he was trying to go around a rock, I still stayed right in the center of his wake and, as I turned left, a big, square, black outline of something loomed out of the fog on my right and we could read the numbers on the license plate of a pickup truck parked on the end of a dock.

The boat I had been following kicked his engines out of gear and hollered back at me,

"Any idea where we are? My radar's been broken for the last five days!"

THE GOVERNOR
AND THE EGG

It was the second ski season of Le Oueff at the gondola in Chamonix, at La Flegere. I had named it "The Dangling Easter Eggs" in my 1962 film. I was still cranking out my feature length ski films on my hand-wind $300 Bell and Howell camera; this was film #14 in a long series of ski films that still continues today. I am now busy working on my 46th annual feature film.

Each individual gondola car was painted a different primary color and, from a distance, they really looked like dangling Easter eggs gliding up and down the mountain in the spring sunshine. The lift went up the sunny side of the valley to one of the best views of one of the most spectacular mountains anywhere in the world, the massive tumbling ice falls of the North Face of 15,000 foot high, Mt. Blanc.

I had extensively filmed "The Egg" the winter before and had shown it all over America. I had now returned to rendezvous and ski with my new friend, the president of the resort.

We met at la Chapeau restaurant for a standard two hour French lunch of Pommes Frittes, steak, salad, and introductions all around the table.

"Warren, I'd like you to meet the Governor."

"Hello, Governor," I replied.

"Morning after."

Lots of people are called governor. No big deal.

He was tall, dark-haired, very handsome, and had a very beautiful wife. Unfortunately, neither one of them could speak English and my French language ability consisted of being able to order an omelette at breakfast, or any other meal for that matter. I would find out, after the very long lunch and half a dozen runs in great corn snow, that they were also excellent skiers.

It was very late in the spring and because of its southern exposure, the lower section of La Flegere was without snow.

Late in the afternoon after half a dozen runs, this forced us to ride down on the gondola. I rode with the Governor, his wife, and the president of the resort. As we neared the bottom, the president said,

"The Governor would like you to come to dinner at his home while you are here in Chamonix."

"Sure, why not," I replied.

"How about Wednesday night?"

Three days later, after a long day of filming good skiers in corn snow, I took a shower, slathered my face and the top of my head with sunburn grease to ease the pain, and started the long drive down to Annecy through Megeve, a very long drive on a very narrow and winding road.

Two hours later, in a pouring rainstorm, I arrived on the outskirts of Annecy. There, I located a Petrol station that was still open and, with the Governor's address clutched in my hand, I used my expert sign language to converse, sign language that was born of many years of not having enough time to learn the foreign languages of each of the many countries in which I'd filmed. Ten minutes of arm waving later, I was given directions to the address with what appeared to me to be a certain amount of reverence and awe.

I was surprised at what I saw when the address I was looking for finally appeared through the slanting rain and the intermittent squeaky scrape of my tired, rent-a-wreck, windshield wipers. In my dim headlights loomed a big iron gate, probably ten meters wide and three meters high.

To the right of it was a sentry box that resembled a phone booth with a peaked roof and no windows. It was painted with five or six inch wide slanting red and white candy stripes.

In the sentry box, standing in out of the rain, was a soldier wearing a gold-buttoned coat with epaulettes and holding a heavy rifle with a fixed bayonet.

This house was being guarded by professionals!

I knew I was in trouble because I was driving a Volkswagen with German plates and I couldn't speak but a few words of junior high school French.

"Se vous Plai? Le mansion Msr. Governor?"

"Oui."

Msr. Miller. Le Guest."

"Oui. Oui!"

Marching stiffly to the far side of the gate, he leaned into it and it swung slowly open. I was now looking at 200 meters of gravel driveway, flanked on either side by immaculately trimmed shrubbery and trees. The lit-up house off in the distance resembled a 47 room hotel I once stayed in in Zermatt.

As I coasted my "Rent a Wreck" to a stop behind a long line of top-of-the line Citroen limousines, three Mercedes, and one Rolls Royce, all with chauffeurs, I knew I was in real trouble. It was dawning on me that this guy really was the Governor. I better think this thing through.

Let's see.

I'm wearing a red and yellow parka that covers my brown and beige tweed suit, a red bow tie with white polka dots, and a nylon wash-and-wear shirt that is sort-of pressed. I guess I shouldn't have worn my after-ski boots. That sheepskin lining is going to get awfully sweaty in there at dinner.

I parked in the dark, traversed the gravel driveway and, as I started up the long wide flight of stairs, I realized they were awfully slippery in the wind-driven rain.

They were made of polished marble.

Knocking on the massive wrought iron and cut glass front door, I waited a few moments. When it swung open, it revealed a highly polished marble-floored foyer with a pair of gently curving stairs that were three meters wide, going up each side of the foyer.

The butler, clad in tails and white gloves, was visibly shaken by my appearance and started talking rapidly in very hushed tones of what sounded like Norwegian with a French accent. He thought I had made a major mistake and belonged in the Youth Hostel down by the Lake. I couldn't understand a word he was saying. All I knew was that he wanted me out of there and quickly.

"Meester Miller!"

A voice shouted from the top of the stairs.

It was the Governor, and with him was my friend, the president of the ski lift company. I think they would have both slid down the bannisters to greet me, if they had not had on their tuxedo and tails.

The Governor was wearing a full set of tails, and draped over one of his shoulders was a handsome red sash full of medals.

I was now really in trouble in my brown and beige tweed suit and my red and white polka dot bow tie with my tall sheepskin-lined after ski boots.

The ski resort president spoke his junior high school English and it wasn't until then that I found out that the dinner party was in my honor. It was a payback because I had sent so many American skiers to Chamonix with my films.

"Yes, your host really is the Governor of the Haute Savoie Province."

"Yes, this is the Governor's mansion."

"Yes, everyone, except you, is wearing their tuxedos or tails."

"Don't worry, Warren, you are a motion picture producer from California, so the other guests expect you to be a little weird."

"Your clothes are no problem. The Governor has an idea."

I followed the two of them into a large library off the reception area, where the Governor lifted the lid to a small walnut and sterling silver chest that was resting prominently on a very beautiful antique table. Inside the chest were half a dozen sashes similar to the one that the Governor was already wearing. They were, however, all different colors, red, green, blue, and white. Alongside the neatly folded sashes were at least two dozen assorted medals. They looked similar to the ones that the Governor was already wearing on his sash and were all about three inches in diameter.

The Governor picked out a red sash to go with my red bow tie and ceremoniously draped it over my head and let it rest on one shoulder. Then he rummaged around amongst his many medals, picked out four or five different ones and, one by one, pinned them on my red sash, starting with the most important medal at the top.

Together, we started climbing up the winding marble stairway to the Grand Ballroom. On the first landing, I glanced at myself in a full length mirror and, as I did, I tripped in my after-ski boots and fell flat on my chest full of medals.

"Yes, I was from California."

"No, I hadn't been drinking."

"Yes, I was living up to their expectations of being weird."

In a few moments now, I would be dining with nine tuxedo or tail-clad men, and nine elegantly gowned and beautifully coiffed women. I began to walk very carefully in my tall after-ski boots, holding my sunburned head high, and wearing my tweed suit with dignity. My hand tied, red bow tie rested about 12 degrees off the horizontal, and I was proudly wearing my sash of the order of Napoleon and the medals signifying my many accomplishments:

The Legion of Merit

French Balance of Payments Booster

Academy of Arts and Crafts Award

And the one with six stars was for perfect attendance in soccer camp all through high school. Or, so I was told.

An incredible, gastronomic, seven course dinner was served and enjoyed by all, during which I had to assume that most of the laughter was at my expense.

The drive back to Chamonix was long on ice and snow-covered roads, and I didn't arrive until about 3:00a.m. By previous arrangement, I had to be on the Dangling Easter Egg lift at 8:00 the next morning with my windup camera and three skiers. I knew the rainstorm last night in Annecy would hit Mt. Blanc and create good powder snow skiing that morning in La Flegere. The ten inches that fell overnight offered a fantastic stage so that I could use the 15,000 foot high Mt. Blanc Massif as a background for many of the scenes in my next movie.

The Governor and his wife missed those first dozen or so powder snow runs with us. When they finally arrived, I found out at lunch that they, and their guests, had spent another hour and a half or so after I left, drinking champagne and laughing at the appearance of the crazy American from Hollywood with his weird tweed suit and polka dot tie.

BOAT ADS AND WHAT THEY REALLY MEAN

With the mud season right around the corner and almost impossible waxing needed for powder at the top, and dirt and wet snow at the bottom, I find my late afternoons being spent reading the Boating magazines instead of the latest and greatest that the ski publications have to offer.

As I read the latest and greatest sales pitches on boating and their accessories, I see a lot of similarity to ski advertising in what the advertisers are trying to sell for the wonderful world of boating.

Advertising agencies all over the world labor long and hard at creating catchy phrases to get you to belly up to the bank and borrow a lot of money to indulge your every fantasy in an Italian styled, 3,127 horsepower, 53 mph, nine gallons to the mile, turbine powered, sun bridge, gimbal mounted drink holder, lethal weapon, called a boat. It comes complete with air bags so you can hit the dock the first 205 times you're learning to dock it.

My job as an interpreter of foreign languages (boat talk is my specialty), is to translate what those coffee drinking, perm haired, gold chained, advertising agency types have written about that boat your wife is trying to talk you out of buying.

DICE THROUGH WATER WITH NARY A CARE

You are buying gas for your boat with a company credit card and you don't own the company.

LAVISH ENTERTAINMENT CENTER.

This means your stove works on either alcohol or electricity when you are tied up to a dock. It also means there are holes cut out for the beer cans to sit in when you are not drinking out of them.

ALTERNATE FLOOR PLAN

The swim platform can also be used to clean fish.

INNOVATIVE KEEL PAD

The chopper gun Operator left his sleeping bag in the cruiser mold and it made the boat draw three more inches, but go 2.82 mph faster.

DINETTE FOR FAMILY MEALS

This is a six-pack of lap towels for eating your frozen dinners.

NOTCHED TRANSOM KEEL PAD

Our mold sagged in the summer sun and we laminated five boats before we found out. Rather than saw them up, we sold 'em and they worked a lot better than the previous ones so now we make all of our boats that way.

INSTRUMENT CLUSTER IN A SEMICIRCLE

It's just like the roulette wheel you were playing when you won the money to buy your boat.

FULLY ENCLOSED HEAD

Applies particularly to cigarette style hulls and means that you should always wear a brain bucket and ice hockey goal keeper's face guard when traveling over 95 mph.

INDIRECT LIGHTING AND PLUSH UPHOLSTERY

You need this in your boat when your are in the mood to finally ask your spousal equivalent to become street legal.

BI AND TRI DIRECTIONAL GLASS

The lay-up guys had a little too much beer on their lunch hour and forgot where they left off when the whistle blew.

CLEGECEL CORE, INCREASED SANDWICH CONSTRUCTION

For lunch, the lay-up crew always eats a half pounder and a large order of fries at Burger King.

OPTIONAL WASHER, DRYER

Depends on whether your clothes are dirty or wet.

REDESIGNED FLYING BRIDGE WITH HELM STATION FORWARD

The manufacturer made a few boats with the helm station aft but all of the party people got in the way and the skipper couldn't see to dock the boat, so they moved it back forward.

MULTI-ZONED AIR CONDITIONING

You can physically move the ventilator in any direction you want the wind to be diverted. If it is blowing.

NEW DESIGN IS A QUANTUM LEAP FORWARD

It accelerates faster and it will cost you a lot more per month to dock it.

FINEST EUROPEAN TRADITION

The boat looks just like the coal scows of the Netherlands. And it will go just about as fast.

BARRIER FREE INTERIOR DESIGN

When you hit a wave, all of the stuff falls out of all of the cabinets and off the counters and shelves and lands in a single heap in the middle of the broken bottles of wine.

FLOATING STAIRWAYS

The stairs are made out of kapok so they do, when the boat doesn't.

ENTERTAINMENT MODULE CONSISTING OF A TV, VCR, STEREO, TAPE DECK, CD PLAYER.

This is a must buy extra accessory for your boat so you can cruise 184 miles to a secluded anchorage in your $114,000 boat. There, you can watch a nine-year-old movie on your VCR while your wife is thawing out a five-month-old frozen casserole she made out of Thanksgiving turkey stuffing and leftover sweet potatoes.

FLO-SCAN, FUEL FLOW METERS

At three and a half gallons of gas per mile and gas at $1.99 per gallon, it is a must so you don't run out of gas or money and not necessarily in that order.

TRAMPOLINE V BERTH

The kids can do their gymnastic exercises while you are trying to sleep in the afternoon sun.

DON'T BE FOOLED BY HER SLEEK LINES AND SENSUAL CURVES.

A boat is a perfect mistress. She takes all of your time, all of your money, doesn't love you, and will perform for anyone on the block.

This is an advertising pitch to sell a 70 mph cigarette hull boat that can handle six people for drinks, four for dinner, and two for sleeping.

Yes, these are all advertising pitches for boating and they make as much sense to a skier as "quad lifts, cap construction, and 20 different angles of release" verbiage means to a boater.

Be sure to read those boat ads a little more carefully so you <u>really</u> know what they mean.

NEW ZEALAND GOATS

In New Zealand in 1968, there were 146 different species of cloven-hoofed animals. One hundred and forty-three of them were deer of one species or another. The other three were sheep, goats, and cattle. This was because there were no padded-foot animals or predators, no coyotes, wolves, foxes, bears, or any animal that could keep the deer population in check. As a result, the deer population had exploded and they were ravaging the grass that the tens of millions of sheep desperately needed. At the same time, the deers' cloven hoofs were causing all kinds of serious erosion problems on the sheep stations.

The deer had proliferated to such an extent that the New Zealand government was offering $3 for every deer tail anyone turned in. A man could become a financially successful bounty hunter if he could afford a helicopter.

He could shoot the deer from the helicopter, haul them out, sell the tails for $3, sell the hides to a tannery, and sell the meat to a company that would jerk the venison and ship it to Europe.

Mel Cain was a very successful bounty hunter who had his own helicopter. His record for a one day kill was 983 deer shot, hauled out, skinned, and butchered.

I met Mel on a rainy, windy winter afternoon in August, in an empty hangar at the Mt.

Cook Air Station. My production crew and I were all standing or sitting around a desk in the corner of the hangar, haggling with the station manager about how and where we could hire a helicopter with a good, safe pilot. And, if we could find one, would we be able to land the helicopter in the Mt. Cook National Park to film on the Tasman glacier without paying a heavy fine?

Because of three weeks of heavy rain up to 9,000 feet, I was already way over budget on the first of 13 television shows that I had contracted to produce, television shows of Jean Claude Killy skiing all over the world after he won his three gold medals in the 1968 Winter Olympics.

The operations manger of Mt. Cook Airlines was on the radio phone, when the increasingly loud rat-tat-tat of a helicopter coming in to land drowned out any chance of further conversation.

Coming in to land?

The helicopter flew right into the hangar and landed alongside of us. With dust and papers blowing all over the hangar, we had all ducked for cover behind the desk as the rotating strobe light under the helicopter swung a lighthouse-like beam around the dark walls.

As the rotor blades started to slow down and the papers and dust began to settle, we slowly climbed out from behind or under the desk to see the pilot sitting in the center of three or four layers of sheepskin. In a rack behind the seat were two carbines. Shutting down his machine was the man we would get to know as Mel Cain, a man we would later trust with our lives.

Within half an hour, we had struck a deal with Mel to fly us up to the Tasman Glacier to film as soon as the weather cleared.

During the negotiations, Mel offered to demonstrate to us that, indeed, he could land us almost anywhere on the glacier. To do that, he would take us mountain goat hunting on the steep cliffs that rose thousands of feet up behind the hotel.

Mel explained to us,

"It isn't too difficult to shoot a mountain goat unless we wanted a trophy head. Finding a big one might take a few minutes longer."

Mel had a friend who worked in the kitchen at the Hermitage, whose father was the local taxidermist. If we wanted to, he could get the heads of whatever we shot mounted for about $30 each. Shipping them to California would be extra. The cook would butcher the game and serve it in the employees' cafeteria at the hotel. Besides all that, Mel would get $3 for each tail.

It seemed to me to be a nice way to spend a rainy fternoon in New Zealand. So, Mel showed us how he would fly from the center of the cockpit. One of us would sit on each side of him with a carbine. Since he would be landing us on steep snow or ice when we would be filming, he suggested that we go after a couple of mountain goats that he called Himalayan Thars. That way, he could show us how he could drop us off and easily pick us up on a very steep hill.

I didn't know a Himalayan Thar from a ball of tar, but the whole exercise seemed like a good way to find out just how good a pilot Mel Cain was.

I was told during lunch,

"About ten years or so, ago, a couple from Germany had imported a pair of these goats, and now the herd numbers about 5000."

After lunch, Killy climbed into the left-hand seat, Mel sat in the center, and I was in the right-hand seat. I had never shot a carbine before, I had never shot from a helicopter before, and I had no idea how big a Himalayan Thar or mountain goat was. I didn't know if one was the size of a small dog or a big cow.

I would soon find out how big one really was.

As we started to lift off from inside the hangar, I became acutely aware that Mel had removed the doors to the helicopter while I was finishing my lunch. There I sat with a carbine cradled in my arm, the roar of the rotor blades in my ears, the fear of God in my heart, and the whine of the engine making my protestations unheard. We climbed rapidly above the Hermitage and soon spotted the first small herd of about ten goats.

As Mel circled for altitude and the helicopter came in close to the cliffs, all of the goats we had spotted immediately scattered, bouncing and sliding down the face of the almost vertical rock cliff, or sliding down on their chests on the ice and snow.

Mel pointed out one that looked a little bigger than the rest and hollered,

"Warren, that one is yours."

"It is?"

I was very lucky, and somehow nailed it with my first shot and then watched it tumble down the cliff for what seemed like forever, at least 1,000 vertical feet.

Mel "articulated the framistram" that controls the rotor blade and we dropped like a safe with the door open. Dropping for what seemed like an eternity, he kicked in the something or other, flipped a couple of switches, and we leveled out and hovered above the first and only game animal I have ever shot that was bigger than a rabbit or a duck.

Geometry and the physical properties of aerodynamics now dictated what came next.

Mel tried to get the helicopter close enough to my trophy so I could step out, wrestle it into the helicopter, climb back aboard, and fly away. No such luck. The cliff was so steep that he couldn't get the helicopter within 150 feet of my trophy animal.

"Not to worry," Mel hollered above the roar of the engine.

"Just throw out the rope."

I hollered back,

"What for?" I had a sinking, what for.

"Just throw out the rope, and then slide down it. When you get to the end of it, I'll rock the helicopter a little bit and start you swinging back and forth. Then, when you swing in next to the cliff, just let go and you can drop right alongside of your trophy."

"Sure, Mel."

"Don't worry. There's a knot near the end of the rope so you'll know when you are there. And besides, the rope's only 150 feet long."

"Mel, why don't you just give me another bullet?"

He did, and I nailed the next goat I shot at. I watched this one tumble down a big snow field to stop on a ledge that was big enough for Mel to at least get part of one landing skid anchored in the snow. That way, I could climb out on the landing skid, step into the snow and wrestle my trophy into the helicopter.

That night, the hotel employees had a fresh goat meat dinner. Mel got his $3 for the tail of a cloven-hoofed animal and I paid my $30 in advance to have the head mounted. Now, almost 30 years later, my mounted Himalayan Thar still hangs in my home in Colorado. Right next to it is the 150 foot, nylon rope Mel wanted me to slide down.

A nylon rope on which Mel had forgotten to tie a knot near the end.

"Hanging on my office wall, with the goat, is the rope that Mel forgot to tie a knot in."

SKI ARTICLES
I'M GLAD I NEVER WROTE

Since 1949, I have produced over 500 movies and collected a lot of articles about sports. Most of the articles, of course, have been about my favorite pastime, skiing. I am always on the lookout for the new and exciting resort, ski lift, or racer to film or write about. In many cases, I was privileged to be there first with my movie camera and my note pad.

However, not everything anyone writes about can be right on target or even close to it. Recently, I was cleaning out my files; among the several thousand articles and rejection slips that I have collected over the years were a collection of articles that I found filed under PREDICTIONS. Here are some of the articles that the skiing world accepted as the gospel when they were published.

WILL ASPEN MAKE IT AS A SKI RESORT?

Dateline: February, 1947. With vacant lots selling for as much as $300, has skiing become too expensive for the common man?

THE FIVE DOLLAR LIFT TICKET? IMPOSSIBLE!

Dateline: Sun Valley, Idaho, 1953. With wooden skis costing as much as $30 a pair and ski poles over $4 a pair, do ski resorts think skiers are mad and will continue to pay such outrageous prices?

SNOWBOARDING IS JUST A FAD

Dateline: Waterville Valley, N.H. 1982. Jake Beertone, slipping and sliding on a sheet of plywood that slightly resembled a surfboard, was arrested when he made the obscene remark,

"Ski resorts will someday let me ride their chairlifts with my new contraption that I call a Snurf."

SKI RACING CAN BE PROFITABLE

Dateline: Race headquarters somewhere in the Rockies, 1994. Ski racing is profitable for the ski club that charges high entry fees, the airlines that fly the competitors to the races, the officials who get free trips to all the races, the caterers who supply all the food to all of the officials, the rental car companies that offer the only way to get to AGONY ACRES where the race is going to be held, and the amateur racers who get all the thousands of dollars in prize money.

HOW TO FIND A REAL ESTATE
BARGAIN IN SKI COUNTRY

Quit looking, because there aren't any.

HOW TO MAKE YOUR SKI VACATION
TAX DEDUCTIBLE

Dateline: Anytime, any destination ski resorts. Attend a medical convention. Never mind you're not a doctor. Have business cards printed up that say, MEDICAL CONSULTANT. Make sure your fanny pack is always full of xeroxes of recent trade articles on hypothermia, sunburn, and angular differential between upper body and thigh where knees most often break. Important stuff like that.

HOW TO ASK THE RIGHT QUESTIONS OF YOUR SKI LIFT PARTNERS

Dateline: Any ski lift, anytime. The most important question to ask is,

"Do you live within commuting distance of where I live so you are not G.U. (geographically undesirable)?" Then you can ask the second most important question.

"Are you single?"

THERE'S BIG PROFIT IN GOOSE DOWN

Dateline: Ping Cho Province, China, 1980. The Chinese government has declared that a suitable substitute for goose down can never be manufactured in Western Countries. With low labor costs for goose pluckers, a spokesman said, "It is impossible to replicate this unique natural Chinese product at a competitive price."

AIRPORT ETIQUETTE WITH SKIS AND BOOTS

Dateline: Any airport, any Friday night in the winter. On your next ski trip, tie a yellow ribbon 'round an old ski bag' and fly, fly, fly, knowing your skis and boots won't get there until three days after your ski vacation is over.

SKI WAXING CAN BE FUN

Dateline: Your condo, somewhere, 1992. It is only fun if you use a credit card and have someone else do it.

MIDWESTERN SKIING CAN BE FUN

No dateline. Because it isn't.

HOW TO BUILD A SKI CLUB CABIN ON THE CHEAP

Dateline: Notel Motel, 1992. You can rent a room in a motel 25 miles from your favorite ski area for about $50 a night. With two double beds, four club members can sleep on the mattresses and four more can sleep on the box springs. Fifty dollars a night divided by eight skiers is only $6.50 each. You can't build a ski clubhouse anymore, anywhere, for that kind of money.

HOW TO ENJOY BEING A RACE
OFFICIAL FOR YOUR SKI RACING
KIDS

Dateline: March 10, 1991. Regardless of their ages, hire a baby sitter and have them be your <u>stand-in</u> <u>race</u> <u>official</u>. Then, you too can have a good time skiing. When the lifts close, you don't have to go looking for your kid because you can always find them in the computer game room.

BIG MONEY IN SKI RESORT STOCKS

Dateline: Wall Street Journal, 1953. Chairlifts are replacing rope tows as a much better way to attract skiers these days. Because of a low investment for construction, combined with a high priced ticket ($4.00 a day) to ride them, this writer predicts a lot of millionaires will be created who purchase ski resort stocks over the next decade.

CHEATER-PROOF LIFT TICKETS ARE
HERE!

Dateline: The Washoe County Jail, 1989. Sly Steve Stunning declared from his jail cell today,

"I only have a couple of modifications to make in the paper I am using in my portable xerox machine and I won't get caught again.

SUN VALLEY OPENS WITH ROUND
SWIMMING POOL

Dateline: Idaho, 1936. Boasting the world's first chairlift, and the world's first round swimming pool, this isolated valley in Idaho promises to be the first place you can take a ski vacation without getting cornered in the pool in your white body by your tan-faced ski instructor.

WILL THE ROPE TOW MAKE SKIERS
TOO SOFT?

Dateline: Woodstock, Vermont, 1935. In this remote Vermont farmyard, the exhilaration of climbing to the summit on your own two skis has been replaced by a one minute ride up on a moving rope, powered by a noisy automobile engine. This writer predicts that skiing on rope tows, instead of climbing, will produce a generation of whimps, rather than the strong mountain men that skiing has produced in the past.

CARE AND FEEDING OF THE
LEATHER SKI BOOT

Dateline: Lech-Am-Arlberg, Austria, 1954. Nothing will ever replace the comfort and the subtle feel of a pair of handmade, tanned cowhide, box-toed, ski shoes. Wearing them, you can always transmit subtle control and sensitivity to your wings of wood.

METAL EDGES ARE TOO DANGEROUS

Dateline: Davos, Switzerland, 1933. After surviving eleven stitches in his leg from a metal edge on his new skis, Wolfgang Bang declared, "They are much too dangerous for any but the most expert racers. And, besides, the snow never gets packed hard enough to need them."

TWO SKI POLES OR ONE?

Dateline: St. Moritz, 1929. This writer predicts that the current fad of a pair of ski poles, instead of one, will never be a success. You absolutely need one long stout pole to sit on to arrest your descent of the steeper slopes above this Swiss Village.

IS THERE A METAL SKI IN YOUR FUTURE?

Dateline: Kufstein, Austria, 1955. Absolutely not! You will never be able to get the subtle, alive, feel of a living piece of hickory, one that was shaped by loving hands into wings of wood.

IS THERE A FUTURE IN THE SKI BUSINESS?

Dateline: Harvard Business School, 1939. The recent invention of the chairlift by an engineer who specialized in the handling of bananas for the Union Pacific Railroad, has presented a test case for a start-up industry.

Choosing a very remote resort in the wilds of Idaho for this experiment in thrill seeking, this graduating class of Harvard feels that there is little chance of anyone being crazy enough to try it. They will have to travel vast distances to risk their life hurtling brains-first down a precipice in the name of fun and games. We predict the entire sport of skiing will be a financial failure.

GORNERGRAT BAHN OPENS TODAY

Dateline: Davos, Switzerland, 1939. With the opening of this mountain cable railway today, skiers, for the first time, can ride to the summit in heated railroad cars. A two mile long cable hauled the first trainload of skiers, and Freidl Furst declared that this is a method of up-skiing that can never be improved upon. The 2,000 vertical foot ride only took 35 minutes, an ascent that takes over two hours on skis.

Recently interviewed in his home in Vorgle, Freidl Furst still maintains, "It will always be the best, the fastest, and the only civilized way to get to the top of a mountain."

BUNGEE JUMPING WON'T REPLACE SKIING

Dateline: Chamonix, France, 1988. This writer predicts this will be the case. The recent 500 vertical meter bungee jump out of the Telepherique proves my point. With jumpers using longer and longer bungee cords, this jumper's cord was six feet longer than it should have been. Funeral services will be conducted as soon as the next of kin can be notified and the body can be recovered.

I'm glad I never wrote any of these articles and my readers probably are, too.

OPTIONS

As my wife and I walked down the dock in Alert Bay, British Columbia, I saw the boat I would someday like to own. Forty feet long, low in the water, a big back yard to fish from, lots of refrigerators and freezers, and controls from the rear fishing deck; everything about it was perfect. The craftsmanship was something you seldom find in a commercially built boat because it was handmade over a five year period by a school teacher from Burnaby, British Columbia.

Len Alton, the boat builder, was the son of a fisherman and Laurie and I spent the rest of the evening with him. All of us agreed that if his boat had two engines, instead of one, we would probably have bought this just-the-right-boat-for-us on the spot.

During the course of the evening, Len spun a few fishing stories, one of which bears repeating here.

Son of a fisherman, he told us how, many years ago, his father saved his own life and the lives of his crew with ingenuity and options.

Today, we complain bitterly when some electronic gear breaks in our boats; or, when we run out of fuel, we call the coast guard and they come and rescue us. Not in the old days. You didn't have a radio, or a depth-sounder, or radar. You had to be a fisherman, a mechanic, an electrical engineer, a meteorologist, a navigator, and yes, maybe even a psychic.

About 60 years ago, Len's father was on a four to five day run in his halibut fishing boat from Alaska to Prince Rupert when their propeller shaft broke. As I have said, in those days they didn't have radios, radar, Loran, or GPS, and the Coast Guard couldn't fly out and rescue you in a helicopter.

His father did have a small stay-sail to reduce the rolling when working in a beam sea. So, the first thing the crew did to try and get the almost 350 miles to port was to make some more sails out of the blankets they had on board, rigging them on the mast and the boom arm that they hung out to the side. A couple of hours later, they began to make some headway with their jury-rigged sails.

Later in the day, with the weather still in their favor, they sawed up part of their boom so they could lash it about amidship and athwartships. They cut the larger section long enough so that it extended about two feet out on either side of the boat. They then rigged crude paddle wheels for each end of what had become a shaft. The paddle wheels were made from the pen boards out of the fish hold. They managed to hold the blades reasonably securely in place with spliced ropes passed through holes drilled in the ends of each pen board. With wooden bearings that they hand carved for the shaft and a lot of grease from the halibut in the hold, they then began to slowly turn the paddle wheels with a rope running around the winch that normally hauled up their halibut lines.

Lucky for them, the weather remained clear with only a slight wind. Looking like a paddle wheel Mississippi River Boat, they managed to make two knots an hour for the next six days. When they got almost to Dixon entrance, which is the ocean passageway to Canada above the Queen Charlotte Islands, they were finally within sight of land. They were, by then, almost out of grease for the wooden bearings for the paddle wheel shaft. They were on very short rations of drinking water when the engine running the paddle wheels finally coughed to a stop as they ran out of fuel. But, they still had more than enough halibut to eat, and were rocking in a gentle seaway and thinking how lucky they were to have gotten so far. In the late afternoon, they saw the first boat they had seen in over a week.

The blankets hung out wing and wing from the gin pole. The weird looking paddle-wheeled fishing trawler and frantic waving by Len's father and the crew finally attracted the other fishing boat. They came alongside, threw a towing line to the side wheeler, and towed them to shelter.

There was a tear of appreciation in my eyes as Len finished the story about his father. He went on to say,

"Today, we complain when there is too much cedar bark in the drinking water that we get free when we refuel, or the mechanic where we have our boat stored for the winter left a greasy fingerprint somewhere on our boat."

"My father always taught me that you can die out there."

"Whenever you are in a boat, always be self-sufficient."

"Always have a safety option of some kind, somewhere else to go, and have an alternate way to get there. No matter where you are, what you are doing, or planning on doing, the weather will change and machinery will break!"

"If you always have an option, you won't die when you're out there."

"If you always have an option, you won't die when you're out here."

IN PURSUIT OF ADVENTURE, AGAIN?

It is cold and windless here in southern British Columbia and raining big, hard, splats of water on top of my sunburned, bald head. I have been rowing this, "call it anything you want," half-full of air, inflatable for the last two hours. With each tug on a pair of oars that were designed for a three foot tall, six-year-old kid, the inflatable bends in the middle a little more. It bends because I have been unable to find the leak that has driven me to near exhaustion. It bends because the engine clamped defiantly and silently on the transom refuses to run, a motor made somewhere in Japan at a design cost of about eight million dollars.

In spite of superb Japanese engineering and robot-driven manufacturing methodology, it still won't run without gasoline in its ten ounce tank. It will, however, run just long enough on that ten ounce tank of gas to get you far enough away from your boat so you can get in a lot of trouble when you don't know your way around, like I don't.

My wife, Laurie, and I had set out from our 20 foot outboard cruiser, "Pursuit," to look for eagles we could photograph on what started out as a clear, cloudless afternoon.

"I thought you filled it up."
"I thought you filled it up."

We said, simultaneously, as I finally figured out that no amount of tugging on the miniature rope would make the miniature engine start without normal size gasoline in the miniature gasoline tank.

The two knot flood tide had swung to a four knot ebb tide as I was sweating, swearing, rowing, and crabbing my way across the Malispina Inlet. In an ever increasing rain squall, we could still make out, in the distance, our 20 foot long, convertible top luxury yacht that we had already driven almost 250 miles in the last four days. The yacht was getting smaller and smaller when I finally managed to get out of the ebbing current and row along close to shore. Now, all I had to do was fight my way through the seaweed and get ashore and try to blow up the folding, collapsing inflatable. With beginner's luck, the foot pump was in the boat, so now I got to exercise my right leg so it could get as tired as my rowing arms.

We were lucky in finding the leak in a place that Laurie could hold her finger over, while I rowed another hour and a half to reach the supposed sanctuary of our 20 foot long yacht.

Our one hour picture taking excursion had turned into about a five and a half hour marathon. In the process, the tide had been dropping rapidly and steadily so our anchorage had lost most of its water. I had to give up rowing the last 100 yards to get to our yacht. Instead I staggered, slipped, and slid on slime and seaweed-covered rocks while dragging the still leaking inflatable. Laurie was, by now, as wet from the downpour as I was from wading, except she was not all covered with green seaweed slime.

Once aboard our grounded 20 foot yacht, I surveyed the tide table, compared it with our aground-on-the-rocks-position, and calculated that it was just past full ebb. It would be three or four hours before the Pursuit would float on its lines again.

I took the other anchor and crawled, slipped, and slid back out until I was in waist deep water. There I wedged it between two rocks, being careful to place it so that when we finally got away from this now rock and moss-covered swamp, the anchor could be pulled free from the other direction.

I staggered back to the boat and unloaded a lot of our gear into the leaky semi-inflated, inflatable to lighten the load in our 20 foot yacht. Having raced sailboats for 20 years, I always carry an old six-part purchase set of mainsheet blocks in my duffel bag. Next, I hooked one end of the blocks to the boat and the other to the anchor line with a carrick bend. With a six times mechanical advantage, I slowly kedged the Pursuit, six feet at a time, into water deep enough so it would float.

Once there, we got to reverse the unloading process and lift all of those boxes of food, books, and supplies up from the dinghy into the boat.

An hour later, the 49 degree water had turned my body blue and created a colorful contrast to the green slime that was all over it. Not to worry. I just climbed up onto the transom of the Pursuit and stood in the rain. With some of Slim Sommerville's marvelous saltwater soap, I lathered up in the continuing downpour.

There is another of Miller's unwritten laws of the sea that whenever you get all lathered up with saltwater soap in a rainstorm while standing on the transom of a small boat, the rain will automatically stop.

On a cold afternoon in southern British Columbia, the law of the sea once again went unbroken and the rain stopped right on cue.

I stood there, naked as a jaybird, coated with saltwater lather and wondering what to do next, when a 63 foot charter yacht ghosted by on the now incoming tide. It was loaded with a dozen Japanese tourists who all had their cameras at the ready.

They, of course, were very happy because a naked soap-covered Caucasian wasn't included in their tour brochure. I didn't want to track soap all through our boat and the bay was too shallow to dive into, so I just stood there and waved back, with soap on my body and egg on my face.

Once they had gotten out of camera range, Laurie came out of hiding and brought me two quarts of fresh water from our six gallon Gatorade thermos, so I was able to rinse off.

Getting out of jams like this in a small boat is a lot easier than getting out of jams in a big boat. In a big boat you can get into bigger jams, but in a big boat you can also take a hot shower after any mess you might get into. In a big boat you can have an afternoon cocktail while you watch from the salon while your skipper and deckhand get your big-monthly-payments-pride-and-joy-yacht out of the mess you got it into.

No one has ever said that powerboating resembles the brochures or the videos that sell the sport. What about Steve Stunning and Grace Good Enough with their 2.5 darling children in darling clothes, with the wind blowing their just-right hairdos that are glued down with hair spray? They wouldn't last 2.5 minutes in the real world of small boat adventure, in spite of ten ounce gas tanks on miniature outboard motors that are designed to drive inflatables at the speed of a slow moving San Juan Island slug.

When I first met my wife, she was afraid I wouldn't like it up in the Northwest. After this first adventure (ordeal), she was the one who whimped out and started talking about her three foot fever. (This is defined as a subconscious urge to have a yacht that is three feet longer, no matter how long your current yacht is). Perhaps she wanted a 23 foot something-or-other with a shower and a toilet that actually flushed.

What sane person, man or woman, would voluntarily climb into a 20 foot boat with a single outboard motor, a small cutty cabin to sleep in, a Coleman stove to cook on, a Coleman lantern to read by, an ice chest to sit on, and a chemical toilet to tinkle in? But since I'm only 6' 2" and my wife is 5' 4", why would we need a bigger boat?

Bigger boats do not make bigger adventures.

But, I am looking at a larger gas tank for the inflatable and maybe a wet suit so I can stay warmer while I wade through the shallows the next time our yacht is aground.

REALITY IN BOAT ADVERTISING PHOTOGRAPHY

The fully loaded 34 foot Cruiser moves away from the dock for only $284,000 or $3,000 a month for 17 years, not counting fuel, insurance, food, bar supplies, and entertainment costs of potential spousal equivalents.

Pictured at the helm is Steve Stunning, who, at the age of 31, is very successful. It is obvious, because he drives a $50,000 car, lives in a home with his own private dock for this, almost the biggest in the neighborhood, boat. Steve and his wife Christina, have 1.7 children. His wife, of course, spends three hours a day in aerobics class and has ironed hair blowing in the wind. She is wearing a *Sports Illustrated* model, bare-hip, bikini that is so small it wouldn't absorb all the oil off the engine dipstick during a routine oil check.

Steve and Christina's 1.7 children have on life jackets and their Nintendo games are stowed below in the open-spaced cabin. The kids are not enjoying this Macho photo session at all. Except that the $300 modeling fee each of them will get will almost pay for that new skateboard they want with the red wheels that light up in the dark.

It is fortunate that Steve got out of the drug business that earned him all of the money to buy this 58 mph dream boat. If he hadn't quit, the helicopter taking the pictures for the advertising agency of "E. E. A. @ S J." (Ego, Expense Account, and Snow Job) would be piloted by a Coast Guard drug enforcement officer with an Uzi instead of a Nikon.

Let's get realistic.

The average owner of a boat like this is 53 years old and is one pound overweight for every one of his birthdays. His name will be Larry or Bruce or Duke or Irving. His tropical tan comes from the ultra violet lamp at the tanning salon. He has had a recent hair transplant at $17.40 for each strand of hair. (He got a quantity discount). The drill they used to plant the hair follicles was oversize and the base of each hair looks like a big black base for a light grey floor lamp. It's hard to keep your eyes off this pockmarked transplant while he is talking to you about gallons per hour, miles per gallon versus revolutions per minute, prop pitch, and cavitation.

Stowed below is Irving's duffel bag full of baseball hats that he always travels with. If he visited the places, he would wear his Maui hat at Aspen, his Vail hat at Gig Harbor, or his Aspen hat at the boat yard on Lake Union. These baseball hats all have a high crown in the front for the logos, sort of a ten gallon hat for tractor drivers who are now boat drivers. He has never been to any of the places listed on his hats because he bought them all out of a mail order catalog.

His wife is one foot shorter than he is, but she is a staunch supporter of the same overweight theory of one pound per birthday. Her name will probably be Audrey or Betty Lou or Bonnie, or even Ethel.

The last time she had on a two-piece bathing suit was at her high school senior ditch day when they all went out to the rock quarry and picnicked, swam, and probably necked a little for the first time.

Now she has a beehive hairdo, glued down with half a can of hair spray for every three hours of lineal boat travel. She is natty, but obese, in her white and blue nautical polyester double knits. They haven't fit since she was a drum majorette in college 29 years ago. Her clothes fit and look like the skin of a Braunschweiger with labels and the price tags still stuck on. All of her nautical clothes have crossed anchors on the lapels. They also have signal flags somewhere on the parka that spell out her name.

Ethel or Betty Lou knows all of the necessary nautical terms, like port quarter, abaft the starboard focsle light, radar, engines, galley, wine cellar, and extended payments. Her real status was her custom-made, mail order, combination mini duffel bag and purse. It is full of credit cards. It has a matching design of signal flags that spell out the name of the boat, "Branch Office." That way Irving and Betty Lou can use the boat as a tax deduction. Her husband, Irving or Duke, was never happier than when a thief stole the mini duffel bag. He didn't even report it because he knew that the thief would probably be spending less than his wife would.

On the bow of the boat is a $2,000 electric winch for the 15 pound anchor that never gets used because our fat, statistical, cruiser captain and his boat are always tied to a dock or, at best, a tow boat because he has run out of gas.

The 110 volt, $7,445 generator in the bowels of the boat has never had to run either, because the boat is cruising flat out all the time and the television can't be turned on. Or, the boat is plugged into the dock and tied up gunwale to gunwale with nine other boats belonging to members of the yacht club that he hasn't seen since the last meeting the night before.

Since the boat is always driven flat out, Captain Irving's guests are hanging on tight and bouncing around. No one can do anything except hang on and watch the fat on the 53 pound overweight skipper and his wife jiggle, just a little out of phase with the chop.

Like sound traveling at 1,100 feet per second at sea level, fat rises and falls at almost that same speed. However, it rises and falls approximately .05347 second later than each individual boat bounce. This is a direct function of the height and fetch of the waves divided by the velocity of the boat over the square root of its water line length.

Mind you, this fat jiggle delay has a variance factor in the time delay resultant when cosmetic surgery enters the equation. This is particularly apparent when the cosmetic surgery has been done on the overweight wife we have been discussing. Thus, the time delay equation of fat rise and fall is obviously altered to read:

TD = time delay of fat rise and fall
WH = wave height
WF = wave frequency
BL = boat length
V = velocity

TD = WH divided by WF multiplied by BL and the square of the boat velocity in feet per second.

So, when you buy that new 34 foot, $284,000 cruiser, forget what you see in the photographs. Forget about planing hulls and tri directional glass; forget about innovative keel pads; forget about clegecel core and increased sandwich construction.

Think instead of how your "fat jiggle delay factor" will appear to your very important guests when you invite them on your Sunday afternoon cruise.

"The light brown pair in the middle are for boating in light chop, with a nine mph wind and a light intensity of f 5.6."

THE IMPERFECT STEWARDESS

The voice of the stewardess came over the loudspeaker in clear and precise tones, sounding exactly like the textbook said it was supposed to, except for a slight tinge of boredom. With perfect enunciation, her speech had been memorized and spoken thousands of times during 30 years of sweaty-palm takeoffs and landings.

As I instinctively blotted out listening to the same old safety speech for the umpteenth time, the other 19 passengers on DC-10 flight number 14723-c began to settle down for what we hoped would be a nonstop flight from Destitute Downs, Delaware, to Broken Spoke, Nebraska.

In over 50 years of flying on commercial airlines, how many times have I heard that same kind of perfect voice giving the same kind of safety speech? It's a speech perfected by expensive psychologists, schooled in the art of trying to convince you that you really are safe way up there in the clouds.

How many times have I wished I could rewrite that perfect speech so it would at least be entertaining enough to listen to and, at the same time, sound a whole lot less scary and intimidating?

Imagine my surprise when our stewardess, Darling Doris Dingbat, was either trying to get a job as a stand-up comedian on her weekends off, or get fired with full retirement benefits for improper use of a microphone.

Here are some of her fractured flight instructions.

"Will the people sitting on the aisle who have their shoulder sticking out in the aisle, kindly pull them in so the pilot can see to back the plane up?"

"For all takeoffs and landings, make sure your tray tables are put away and your seat backs are in their full, upright and most uncomfortable position."

"In the event of a water landing anywhere in Nebraska, be sure to study the 43 page safety manual in the seat pocket in front of you. Study it carefully so you can learn how to put on your life jacket without waking up your neighbor."

"In the unlikely event of a sudden loss in cabin pressure because one of your kids opens a side door, oxygen masks will automatically drop out of the roof directly above you.

"I hope!"

"On the outside chance that you have one or more of your kids riding in those very expensive seats next to you, make sure you get your own oxygen mask on first. Once you can breathe normally, if there are any extra masks, try to get one on each of your kids before they stop breathing and begin to turn blue. Then, just continue to breathe normally until a crew member advises you to stop."

"If you are riding in the mileage plus, freeloading, upgrade seats, for lunch today, you will have your choice of either Zucchini Lasagne or a

Macaroni and Cheese casserole, with a slice of our new one-grain bread. We will also be serving all the free vintage wine you can drink from those new recyclable and biodegradable cartons. Or, if you are stuck in the back in the cheap seats, you will get a bologna sandwich with mayo, a chocolate chip cookie, and a sort-of fresh glass of supposed mountain spring ice water."

"Soft drinks are free for everybody. It doesn't matter how many free miles you have earned flying while you were working for old Amalgamated Industries. That includes all of those trips you claimed as a business expense flying first class. But, we know you were flying coach and pocketing the refund."

"Wine, whiskey, bourbon, scotch, and gin are all free up front. You guys and gals back there in the cheap seats are, once again, going to get stuck for $4 a pop for the hard stuff."

"Since this plane is now going to be late due to the fire in the #3 engine, I have some gate information for your connecting flights, if and when we finally get to our Nebraska destination."

"You didn't know about that little old fire did you? I think the captain did a good job of faking you out with that story about some unusual air turbulence."

"Once we land, which we eventually have to do, wherever we happen to be, we will taxi to either gate C-38 or A-4. If you are going on to San Bernardino, your connecting gate is F-9. If you are going on to Reno, your gate is C-1. And good luck with your marriage or divorce, whichever it will be this trip. If you are going north to Calgary, your gate will be B-39. If you are going on to Denver, Colorado, you will have to go outside the terminal building, grab a cab on the lower level to the old Metropolitan Airport, and check the TV screens in their lobby. Allow 30 minutes for your cab ride and, while you are riding across town, think about firing your travel agent for giving you such lousy connections."

"Keep your seat belts tight and low across your waist. Unless, of course, you are too fat. Then tighten your seat belt wherever you can get it completely around you. Leave it that way until the entire flight crew has deplaned because we all know you will plug up the aisle on your way out."

"Check the seat pockets in front of you to make sure you or any previous passengers have not left any valuables behind. While you're at it, check your hip pockets, your front pockets, and your coat pockets, too."

"Please stay seated until the plane comes to a complete stop and the seat belt sign has been turned off. We don't want anyone falling down and suing us."

"I'd _like_ to welcome all of you to Honolulu. However, we have just landed in Broken Spoke, Nebraska."

"The seat belt sign won't be turned off for quite awhile because you have just landed at Nebraska's new International Airport. The runways here are being built with Bill Clinton's value-added tax dollars. All 11 runways are being built seven miles long to accommodate the supersonic jets of tomorrow. If those politicians in Washington would let us join the European Economic Community, we could be landing in a supersonic Concord today. If you had been flying from Paris that is. Now that we are finally safely on the ground, you can relax because we will be taxiing for approximately 35 minutes."

"On behalf of the management of this airline and the personnel who got you here safely, we want to again thank you for flying the airline of tomorrow, today. We also hope that, if and when you ever think about flying again, you will go Greyhound and leave the driving to them."

"And, as you climb into your car for the most dangerous part of your journey, don't forget our motto! If we don't get you there on time, it's no big deal. You're alive and your big deal will probably wait until you get there."

"Will the people on the aisle please pull their shoulders in so the pilot can see to back up."

SKID CHAINS

Long before the invention of four on the floor, four wheel drive, mini-vans, air bags, and ABS brakes, someone had already invented FRONT wheel drive cars. Before that, there was an archaic piece of frozen, unmanageable hardware called skid chains.

A good pair of skid chains used to cost about $8, and if you skied anywhere in the west you had to have a pair of them stored somewhere in your car. Driving up from near sea level to go skiing, you always drive through an elevation where the rain begins to turn to slush and then higher up, it finally turns to snow.

At the elevation where the storm is the wettest, the State Highway Patrol will post an armed guard and not let you drive on up to the ski resort without putting on your skid chains.

Having been in this skid chain application situation many times, I long ago learned to do as the Highway Patrol tells me to, sometimes even beating them to the decision.

Some years ago I was trying to sell a short film to my friend, Dick Kohnstamm, at Oregon's Timberline Lodge. I had flown up from Los Angeles and arrived in Portland about midnight, just in time to get the last discount rental car available and drive halfway up to Mt. Hood. At about the 3,200 foot elevation, freezing rain made my decision for me. I spent the night in the Notel Motel in the small town of Rhododendron. The sign out front said "Morally clean, luggage required".

The next morning, there was six inches of very wet snow on my rental car. Rather than wallow in the mud at the chain control station, I decided to put the chains on the car right where I had parked it the night before.

No big deal. I laid the chains out on the ground behind the rear wheels and backed the car over them, just as I had done dozens of times in the past. Then, I fought the chains up over the top of the wheels, laid down in the wet snow so I could hook everything up, and was ready to go.

The rest of the drive to Timberline Lodge was without incident. The parking lot, however, had two and a half feet of new, powder snow in it. Heavy, wet, northwest powder snow. Not a problem with my rental car skid chains on tight.

It was fun making first tracks in the parking lot, but when I came to a stop I found it was impossible to open the car door. The new snow was that deep.

Since this was a selling trip, I was wearing a sport coat, slacks, necktie, loafers, and would be carrying my briefcase. I rolled down the window, climbed out, and sunk up to my knees in the deep, wet snow. I packed down some of it with my loafers and soon had a place big enough to open the door. I grabbed my briefcase, rolled up the window, and wallowed towards the lodge in the tracks the car had left.

The film discussion took a couple of hours and during the two hour lunch that followed, another six inches of wet, heavy snow had fallen. As only it can in the Northwest!

As I said good-bye to Dick, I could barely see my rental car that was now almost completely buried in the new, wet, heavy, wind-driven Northwest snow.

Ten minutes later I had scraped the snow and ice off the windshield, had acquired two frozen feet, and was ready to charge out of the parking lot wearing my neck tie and my top-of-the-line skid chains.

I was ready to leave, but the car wasn't.

Nothing I could do with the throttle would make the car move. I rolled down the window and discovered that the front wheels were spinning instead of the back ones.

I had put the skid chains on the back wheels.

It was front wheel drive.

Dumb.

I sat there with the engine running and the heater on high for a few minutes, while I tried to figure out how to get my skid chains moved to the front wheels without any help and a least two hours of shoveling.

Through the fiercely blowing snow, I spotted a pickup truck with its engine running. It is not easy to stagger a couple hundred feet or so through three feet of new snow in a pair of loafers and wearing a sport coat and tie, needing help, feeling dumb...really dumb.

The driver looked to me like someone who would help me because he was obviously a mountain person: he had a broom sticking up in the back of his pickup. There was a shotgun, a carpenter's level, and a trout rod on the rack in the back window. A black labrador was sitting in the passenger seat wearing a yellow bandana, and the driver had a nine inch long ponytail and ten inch long beard. He was eating a peanut butter sandwich and reading the local tree hugger environmental magazine, feeding bites of his p-butter sandwich to his dog.

When I knocked on his window, he rolled it down about three quarters of an inch and said,

"I been watchin' ya. See you're stuck."

"I sure am. Will you help me get unstuck?"

"Where ya from?"

"California."

In disgust, he quickly rolled up his window.

I hollered above the howling wind,

"Would $20 convince you to help me get my car unstuck?"

I waited while he thought about it. Then his window slowly rolled down again.

"For two $20 bills, I'll hitch a rope to your car and drag you out to the plowed road. But only if you promise me one thing."

"What's that?"

"When you head down that highway, make sure you stay in California where you belong. Don't never come back up here to Oregon."

"Up here, we're real skiers!"

---

skid/'chain (Webster's dictionary)
    an iron shoe or clog attached to a chain and placed around a wheel that is frozen, unmanageable and supposed to supply traction to an automobile tire when it comes in contact with ice covered asphalt. If you can get it on a tire.

THE CATHEDRAL OF THE GODS

The sky above the village was slowly changing from grey to the pale blue of dawn. In the street below my apartment, the apprentice baker peddled by on his bicycle, dwarfed by his huge, woven wicker basket full of delicious smelling rolls for the hotel down the street.

I had already been up for half an hour packing all of my camera gear in yet another rucksack similar to the many that I have worn out during the last 25 years.

My appointment was to rendezvous at the helicopter pad at 7:00a.m. with our guide, our three skiers from Idaho, and my cameraman.

I was the last to arrive and handed my skis and tripod to Ricky Andenmatten. As I climbed in and buckled up, there was anticipation in the air so thick you could cut it with a knife.

The pilot, who only spoke French, started throwing switches and doing things so that the turbine engine began to wind up and scream its high pitched whine. Now, the huge rotor blades above us began to bend upward from the center as the increasing rpm told us we were going to be airborne any moment.

Then the normal shudder of the helicopter on takeoff began, as if to signal that this incredible machine didn't really care too much about gravity when it was running at the right rpm.

The pilot now did whatever he was supposed to do with the controls, the tail lifted up, and we began to move forward and claw our way upward in the cold, thin, high mountain air.

Since I owned the film company and was paying for everyone's ride, I got to sit in the front seat to the left of the pilot and keep my movie camera running during most of the flight. That way, I would capture all of the necessary scenes for the editor to work with when we got back to my studio in southern California.

In the back seats was our Zermatt Guide, Ricky Andenmatten, my other cameraman, Don Brolin, and skiers, Bob Hamilton, Pat Bowman, and John Reveal.

As this magic machine climbed up towards the Theodel Pass that led from Zermatt to Italy, the sun was already etching beautiful, angular shadows across the untracked snow and the tumbling ice fields that, in places, are over 1,000 feet deep.

To our right, the Matterhorn once again assumed its rightful role as the Altar in this vast Cathedral of the Gods.

Barely 15 minutes after we left the village, we landed gently in deep, powder snow on the northeast shoulder of Monte Rosa. The 15 minute flight would have taken us 24 hours if we had climbed it on our skis.

And now it was time for Don Brolin and me to begin our film making job. We did it with all of the skill and knowledge that had been honed and refined during thousands of descents on skis with camera in hand. Between us, we have skied and filmed all over the world during the last 45 years.

During the next six hours, under our direction, Bob, Pat, and John leaped over crevasses, rapelled down ice blocks, and carved endless turns in untracked powder snow.

Our guide, Ricky, kept us alive with his knowledge of where the ice bridges and crevasses would be, where we could ski, and where we could die.

Gradually, we began to get the sequence "in the can." We would film them making a dozen or so turns and stop. We would then put our gear back in our rucksacks and ski down to somewhere below them and stop and set up our cameras for another angle, while they would wait for us to compose the shot. Then, following Ricky's expert advice, I would tell them where to turn and where not to turn.

About 2:00 or 3:00 p.m., Ricky said,

"I have a great surprise for you guys. Follow me. But be sure to stay in my tracks."

He then skied on down below us for three turns and disappeared down a slope that led right into a crevasse, hollering,

"Follow me."

He was slowly and timidly followed by John, Pat, Bob, and Don. I have always been suspicious of surprises on high mountain glaciers, especially when people disappear into a crevasse! So, I took longer than usual to put my camera away and then I slowly sideslipped down to join them.

At the bottom of the powder snow slope that led down into the crevasse, everyone was standing in silent awe. Except for me; I was scared to death! As my eyes slowly got accustomed to the darkness, I became even more frightened. We were standing inside the beginning of a half mile long, 40 meters wide, 20 meters high, tunnel of ice. At the far end, the sun was sending brilliant, beautiful slivers of fractured rainbows in every direction. Beside us, a ten meter wide, one meter deep river of pale grey-green, almost white, icy water was loudly tumbling its collection of rocks as it rushed noisily by.

Overhead, the massive ice blocks of the glacier were leaning together, forming a true "Cathedral of the Gods." The slanting ice walls were 40 or 50 feet high and had been undercut along their base by the swiftly flowing river.

Ricky was the only one who didn't appear to be scared when he said, "We can ski along this ice ledge by the river. It's only about a meter wide, so be careful. This ice is a lot harder than any icey snow you are used to skiing on. Be sure not to slip and fall into the river. If you do, you'll get sucked under the ice and drown before I can rescue you."

This seemed like an appropriate time to ask Ricky what I thought was a very logical question.

"What makes you think this ice won't cave in on us while we're down here?"

He had a logical answer.

"Warren, what makes you think it will?"

Ricky had probably been down here before, he knew what he was doing, and he wasn't going to risk his life just to show off for us.

As I inched slowly along on the ice ledge, I was spellbound by the hanging icicles, the dripping water, the pale grey-green water rushing by, and the many different colors of the ice. I was really scared by the occasional rumble and thunderous explosion coming from the movement of some other block of ice somewhere else in the vast glacier. The noise of its movement was amplified and transmitted all the way to where I cowered.

About half a mile later, we emerged into the brilliant light at the end of this unbelievable Cathedral of the Gods, more beautiful and for me, more spiritual than any of the many cathedrals I have visited in my lifetime of world travel.

When we finally began sidestepping to get up into the brilliant sunshine and powder snow on top of the glacier, it was a lot later than I thought. We had spent over an hour traversing only a half mile under ice that was at least four or five hundred feet thick.

Now, we would have to hurry so we could catch the last gondola before it left to take us down to the village at 6:00. Led by Ricky, everyone took off in a long, high speed traverse for the last mile or two.

Ahead of us and slightly off to the right, the Matterhorn showed us yet another of its many moods in the late afternoon sun. To the left of this incredible mountain was the Theodel Pass that leads to Italy, and a little further to the left was Monte Rosa. I could still see our tracks etched by the late afternoon sun, tracks that we had filmed seven hours and five or six miles ago.

Our skiers had left graceful turns, while Don and I had left long traverse and kick turn tracks as we moved a lot less skillfully from camera set-up to camera set-up.

Ricky, John, Pat, and Bob had very quickly skied away from Don and me. We were laden down with our rucksacks full of about 50 pounds of cameras and tripods. I also had an extra 20 birthdays to carry around, so that always adds a certain amount of weight to a day's work on a glacier. I was lurching along last in the wet tracks of slushy snow, when a flash of light caught my eye way off in the distance near the top of the Theodel Pass.

I stopped, and was barely able to make out two tiny dots carving figure eights in the late afternoon corn snow. They were headed for one of the high mountain huts to spend the night.

It was really a beautiful sight. So I took off my rucksack, unhitched my tripod, set it up, got out my camera, mounted it on the quick release, hooked up the battery belt, spun the prism so I could see through the view finder, focused the lens and then zoomed it to the maximum focal length telephoto available, 285 millimeters.

What I then saw close up was truly unbelievable.

The tracks they were leaving in the back-lit corn snow were almost black.

As I was reaching for the on switch on my camera, a thought occurred to me.

I've been recording scenes like this since 1949, so I could share them with millions of people.

So, I just watched these two skiers make 109 turns, while my own party of skiers traversed on ahead to the gondola.

If I missed that last gondola, so be it.

I saved that beautiful scene just for me. No one will ever see it. Nor will anyone ever see any pictures of the interior of my own private Cathedral of the Gods.

I never did turn my camera on.

PROPER PROPS

It is early evening and the sea is very calm. My wife, Laurie, and I are following Bruce and Becky Barr in their 12-year-old, 32 foot Bertram sport fishing boat. They are commercial fisherman and fisherwoman by trade and Llama and Alpaca breeders by speculation. They have also experienced almost every adventure known to man or woman on the water, in an airplane, on skis, in a hang glider, on a float plane, or on a motorcycle.

We are beginning a cruise in our 28 foot Regal on our first trip up the outside of Vancouver Island. Laurie has looked forward to this trip with her constant companions, fear and trepidation, because we don't have radar, GPS or Loran. But we do have a radio and a lot of charts and Bruce is a good guide. He has 12-year-old radar on his 12-year-old boat and he has almost assured us that it works most of the time.

We have an awful lot of stuff on our boat for the two month cruise we are taking through the waters of British Columbia, but even so it seems to take a very long time to get our boat up on a plane, almost 2 minutes and a lot more rpm than I remember from last year's cruising. Bruce's boat cruises slower than mine, so I have to get on and off a plane continually to stay behind him.

About the umpteenth time I shove forward on the throttle to get back up on a plane to catch up with Bruce, the rpm come up but the boat doesn't. The starboard engine is not delivering power to the prop. I rev it up two or three times and Laurie looks at me with that "I thought you could fix everything look." I feel like the dumbbell that I am when it comes to yet another newly broken mechanical, assumed to be, life-threatening experience.

I can't get the boat to go over 12 mph as Bruce is pulling away into the growing darkness. His radar might be working but his running lights aren't.

I don't have the slightest idea what is wrong. Maybe some kind of a something has broken somewhere? But there was no loud bang, the tach is registering O.K., and I don't think the engine has a clutch.

"Laurie, I just don't know what's wrong!"

"Bruce must have his radio turned off because I can't raise him."

"Chances are he will look back before long and see we are not right behind him and come back and help us."

"I sure hope so."

"We can always go back to Roche Harbor on one engine and spend the night."

"Hey, he's finally turning around."

Ten minutes later Bruce and Becky are alongside.

"What channel are you on?"

"Thirteen."

"I'm on 72."

Once we got the channels right and were able to explain to Bruce what happened, he said, simply, "You spun a prop. We'll stop in Oak Bay instead of going clear to Victoria tonight and fix it in the morning."

At 10:30, in the nearly dark of the Northwest summer twilight, we are finally ready to try and tie up on the weather side of a dock in Oak Bay. A 25 knot wind is blowing us against the dock, so we put out lots of fenders and get lined up and drift down alongside of Bruce's boat.

No problem docking.

A phone call to an 800 number clears us with Canadian customs, we get our entry numbers, write them out on a sticky back Post-it, stick it onto the windshield, and go to bed.

After breakfast, I found out just how cold the water is in this part of the world. The wind is still blowing 25 knots and the waves are just high enough to wash over the swim step. The water is 11 degrees below zero, or so it seems, because I now get to spend about a zillion hours lying down on the wave-swept, swim-step reaching down, elbow deep in the cold water and trying to undo all 8 of the flanges on the washer that holds the nut that keeps the prop on the shaft. (I found out later that it's only necessary to bend over 2 or 3 of the flanges, not all 8 of them.) By the time I get them straightened out, my hands and my arms up to my elbows are so cold I am getting an ice cream headache all over my body.

I had wisely attached fishing line to the screw driver I was using because I couldn't feel my fingers and didn't want to drop it. The waves were making it impossible to see anything under the water because of the turbulence, and I had to do everything by feel. It seemed like it took a day and a half to get the prop off. Finally, I limped up to a shop on the dock with the prop and was told that the closest place to get a prop fixed was in Nanaimo. But, the guy in the shop thought he could find a replacement a lot closer if I had enough float left on my credit card.

Two hours and $197 later, the replacement prop arrives.

Now I have to reverse the 44 degree water, upper body immersion, prop replacement, drill.

By 1:00, we're on our way with me steering with my elbows because my arms and hands have absolutely no feeling in them.

With discretion the better part of bravery, Bruce opted for us to spend the night tied up to the dock in Victoria instead of going on up the outside of Vancouver Island to Barkley Sound, a distance of about 80 miles. Our overnight in Victoria is a story all by itself that I will tell another time.

By the next morning, I am almost thawed out as we top off our fuel and head outside and north towards Bamfield in Barkley Sound.

About an hour out, we see our first Orcas. A few minutes later, the wind starts and then the drizzle starts until the visibility decreases to about 200 yards. I am glad I am following someone with radar. I still am having the problem of the boat dropping down off a plane and then having to speed up so that I could keep Bruce in sight, yet not run over him.

Barkley Sound is about 80 miles up the outside of Vancouver Island above the Strait of Juan De Fuca opening to the North Pacific Ocean. This was Laurie's second trip outside and my first. There can be a false sense of security when you know that you are following people who have been here dozens of times, like Bruce and Becky have. Laurie had a head full of bad memories from a trip 25 years ago with a captain and a crew that shouldn't have left the dock.

An hour and forty minutes out of Victoria, the "this time I know what is wrong sound" of another prop spinning, howled in our ears as we came down off a plane.

Same problem, only this time another 40 miles of open ocean with pouring rain, 200 yards of visibility, and a 15 mph headwind was between us and a safe anchorage. This time, we could only go 10 mph. Fortunately, we were on the same radio channel as Bruce, so he slowed down and stayed with us.

He had the radar and could have charged us anything he wanted to pilot us to safety.

Four hours later, we rounded the corner of Cape Beale and turned into Barkley Sound, then took another right turn a few miles later into Bamfield.

After we tie up at the Government dock, I once again got to remove a spun prop. Only this time, it was a lot easier because I had only turned over two of the 8 flanges and there wasn't a 25 knot beam wind blowing while I crouched on the swim step with one foot waves washing over me.

With the dinghy launched, Bruce and I drove it across the bay with both of the spun props to Ostrom's combination fuel dock, boat repair shop, fishing tackle, general store, gas station, smoking allowed everywhere, repair shop, and garage.

Optimism is a must when you cruise in this part of the world.

Standing there in the machine shop, my enthusiasm began to wane when the mechanic said, "Nope, can't fix 'em here. Ain't got a big enough press. Closest place you can get them things fixed is down in Nanaimo. Bus goes to there, but you got to get to Port Alberni to get it. 'Bout 40 miles to Alberni and another 40 to Nanaimo. Bus'll leave sometime tomorrow mornin'."

It's 4:30 Friday afternoon. It would be impossible to get a spun prop fixed in any major seaport in the world on Friday afternoon at 4:30.

Inside the fishing tackle part of the General store was the most "turn back the clock" marine hardware and fish supply store I have ever been in. When I saw a 1934 calendar hanging on the wall, I held out little hope of this being the place to ever get my props fixed.

"We just save them calendars and use 'em again cuz the right days come around every few years."

I staggered back outside after inhaling second hand smoke from 5 salmon fishermen who were buying a little bit of food and a lot of cigarettes for their next three weeks at sea.

I chatted it up with a logger in a beat-up pickup truck and found out he was driving to Nanaimo that night to get his chainsaws fixed.

Sure, he knew where the prop shop was and he would drop them off for me.

"Couldn't do it until Saturday morning if that was O.K."

I went back inside and had Grace call the prop shop in Nanaimo.

"Here, you talk to him. This is Joe."

"I don't suppose you work on props on Saturday do you?"

"Of course we do! This is summer and there's no work here in the winter."

"If I got my props to your shop first thing Saturday morning, could you get them back on the bus to Port Alberni on Saturday afternoon?"

"Don't know why not."

"A deal. Do you want my credit card number, or a blank check."

"Neither. I don't know how much they'll cost to fix, or how much the bus'll be, so I'll just include a bill in the box when I send 'em back up. Is that O.K.?"

Out front, I gave Clyde, the logger in his pickup truck, the two props. I had taped a $20 bill to one of them for his trouble.

"I only live six or seven miles from the prop shop and I'll get them in there first thing in the morning. Is that O.K.?"

"It's all set at the prop shop; go for it."

Back inside, the owner of the machine shop told me,

"A friend of mine in Port Alberni is coming down for a Saturday night party and she will pick up the props from the afternoon bus and have them back in Bamfield between 4:30 and 5:00 Saturday afternoon."

"Sounds incredible to me, but if she makes it I'll buy a case of beer for your party."

Then Bruce said,

"Let's leave your boat tied to the dock tomorrow, go out and catch some salmon in our boat, come in, get the props, install one of them, and the next day we can go over to Ucluelet for a couple of days and catch some more fish."

That night we stood on the dock after dinner with Bruce's butane heater providing a lot of warmth. Laurie disappeared aboard our boat and returned with a box of marshmallows, some Graham crackers, and Hershey bars. We roasted the marshmallows in front of the butane heater, squashed them between the graham crackers with a piece of the Hershey bar, and made Schmoores out of them just like we did when we were little kids.

Next day, we nailed a lot of salmon with Bruce's expert guidance. While I enjoyed catching them and learned a lot from Bruce on how to do it, in the back of my mind was the knowledge that it had to be impossible to get my props fixed so easily. Forty miles on a dirt road to Port Alberni, 40 miles to Nanaimo, delivery of the props first thing Saturday morning by a tired logger, fix the props and get them back on an 11 o'clock bus for Port Alberni. Would the person who was coming to Bamfield pick them up? How many variables can you crank into one 24 hour period?

Late that afternoon while Bruce, Becky, and Laurie cleaned the salmon, I drove the inflatable over to see if the whole magical prop repair thing had happened.

"They've been here about an hour, but I'll need a couple of dollars more for all of the telephone calls."

The unbelievable had happened.

Back at the boats, no one could believe it.

I decided to put one of the props back on before we barbecued the salmon filets.

When Bruce went to the controls on my boat to raise the out-drives closer to the surface so I could put the prop back on without freezing too much of my body, he said,

"Have you turned on the circuit breaker so you can use your trim tabs?"

"Oops."

"That's why it has been taking so long to get your boat up on plane and why you spun the props."

DUMB!

(Editors note: During this fishing trip, Becky was fighting cancer and had just finished extensive radiation treatments. She was wearing a chemotherapy pump, had less hair than I do, and had the greatest, "everything is wonderful, spunky, attitude." We lost her a year later, after countless surgeries. Fishing isn't the same.)

"I then spent a zillion hours on the swim step in 47 degree water, trying to change the prop.

SURPRISES

The torrential rain beating on the deck of our small boat woke us early this morning. As I unzipped the canvas tarp on the afterdeck and looked up at the surrounding mountains, I could see the low, dark rain clouds moving rapidly from the southeast. Turning on Channel One Radio, the forecast was marginal for today's trip to Alert Bay from Viner Sound.

"Wind from the southeast at 25 to 40 mph with occasional heavy rain."

With this wind direction, we should be protected from any big waves, except for the short passage across Blackfish Sound and the five or six mile downhill ride into Johnstone Strait. This would be after we rounded Pearse Islands and headed for Cormorant Island and the sanctuary of Alert Bay.

We had spent a delightful evening, anchored quietly by ourselves in Viner Sound and fell asleep looking forward to a limit in our crab pot the next morning. We had run low on our clams and our salmon fishing without a guide was not going very well.

While Laurie was cooking breakfast, I rowed the inflatable over to haul up the crab pot and was not disappointed as I took out our limit of the biggest ones. She cleaned them on the swim step while the oatmeal was getting to the just right consistency and I busied myself stowing gear for the 35 or 40 mile journey to Alert

Bay. We were looking forward to getting there for a visit to the U'mista Indian Cultural Center.

After cruising together for five weeks on a 28 foot boat, the intricate dance of doing things that close together, yet independently, gets all of our chores done in a short time. About 30 minutes after breakfast, the crabs were cooked and the dinghy and the crab cooker were stowed. Time to turn on the blower in the engine compartment. Laurie came topside immediately, got behind the wheel, and fired up both engines, as I climbed around our canvas cabin to the bow and began to haul in the 60 feet of rope, chain, and anchor. (My next boat will definitely have a power anchor winch.) With hand signals from me, she drove the boat in the direction of the anchor line. I got it aboard and stowed, and took over driving the boat down the calm waters of Viner Sound towards Hornet Passage. Laurie went below to check everything in the galley just in case we had to cross a beam sea enroute to Alert Bay. We had looked at our charts during breakfast and thought we would be able to cruise in the shelter of nearby islands almost all of the way.

Surprise.

Crossing Knight Inlet, we were forced to slow down to about five or six mph, as we rocked and rolled in four foot seas on a beam reach. (Our normal cruising speed is about 25 to 30 mph.) Once across the inlet, I noticed two boats anchored in the cove of Warr Bluff by the Indian Village of Mamalilakula. We should have headed in there, anchored, and ridden out the storm.

We didn't.

But, fortunately, a week or so before, I had installed a pair of teak handles for Laurie to hang onto in bad weather. They still have her hand prints squeezed into them from white knuckling it across Knight Inlet. All the way across, I had to keep reassuring her that I wouldn't put myself in a life-threatening situation, so why would I put both of us in one.

Finally, in the lee of Village Island, we cruised in almost glassy water for the next ten or fifteen miles. In Blackfish sound, I was very surprised when I saw several commercial salmon fishing boats heading the same direction we were. I assumed they had full loads and were heading into Alert Bay to sell or transfer their loads to the fish buying tender who would then haul their catch to Vancouver for processing.

Wrong.

They couldn't set their nets because the seas were getting so rough and the wind was blowing so hard. This commercial salmon opening requires that the small tender who ties the net to the beach or the buoy must be rowed by hand. No motors allowed.

By now, the waves were above the five foot mark with a very short fetch. This was made worse where a tidal current of six or eight knots slammed into stationary water and the wind was blowing in still another direction. I had never before experienced five foot seas with only a 25 foot fetch, a little wobbly for a skiff as small as most of these commercial ones were (about 15 feet). They were hauling in their nets and heading for shelter.

Since they are only allowed to fish for a very limited number of days a year, one day of bad weather can dramatically affect their boat payment schedules. But the smart skippers were still heading for shelter. It is better to have a boat to still owe money on than NOT have a boat that you still owe money on.

We passed a couple of them that were still trying to set their nets between Plumper and Pearse Islands, when the full force of the rapidly increasing wind and seas really hit us.

I thought, what I'm doing is kind of dumb, but I had enough horsepower in my two engines so I could stay on the face of a wave in a following sea. I wasn't about to turn around and head into waves of this size and wind blowing this hard. Now my wife was really white knuckling it as I kept reassuring her that the waves were O.K. and the wind was only blowing about 20 (we found out later it was blowing a steady 46, with gusts of 63 mph).

When you are on the helm and have complete control of a boat, it's a lot different than when you are a scared passenger, and I understand that.

The following seas were growing higher, the farther we got out into Johnstone Strait, until I began to worry as we headed towards two colliding tides. In a trough between waves I couldn't see over, each wave had a fetch of just about a boat length. In the center of one tidal disturbance, I bounced through a lot of waves where the bow and stern would be on a crest and there would also be a crest amidships and that's in a 28 foot boat. The waves would be four or five feet high and breaking. This made the fetch less than 14 feet. I only went through one of those tidal messes and then managed to steer around the rest of them. That six miles of riding waves in a 28 foot boat was a real thrill for me and stark terror for Laurie. I don't like it when she gets frightened; for that matter, I don't like it when I get frightened, but there was nothing to do now but keep going and get into Alert Bay. My years of sailing and surfing, as well as having more confidence in the boat and its motors, made it fun for me rather than the terror she was experiencing.

As we rounded the corner and began to fall in the lee of Cormorant Island, we could finally start looking for a place to tie up. With no prior experience in this anchorage and no way to examine a chart in the wind, rain and sea, I still didn't want to go to the downwind end of the bay. If I did, I would have to somehow manage to turn around and beat to windward through the big waves to what would then be our appraisal of the right dock.

We decided to try to dock at the first place that looked even remotely possible for us to handle. The wind was blowing 53 mph at about 30 degrees away from the dock, and the tide was running at about four or five knots parallel to the dock. (Of course, she didn't know that.)

We made a quick "U" turn into the wind as soon as I thought we could handle the big waves and the landing, and eased right in there and tied up like we knew what we were doing. We were soon helped by three of Canada's finest Coast Guardsmen. They had been following our progress through the howling wind and waves from their station on the bluff with their binoculars. As we doubled and tripled up all of our lines they told me, "The wind has been blowing a steady 48 mph and there have been gusts that hit 63 mph in the last couple of hours. And you say you are from Colorado and your boat was built in Florida?"

They were shaking their heads.

(Isn't there a saying about someone that looks after fools?)

Just dumb.

We thanked them for their help and took a chance that our boat wouldn't blow away while we went to lunch. This would be the first hamburger, fries, and chocolate shake we have had in five weeks.

Returning to the boat an hour later, we discovered that the wind and current were so strong that two of the eye splices in the mooring lines had pulled out. Anticipating problems, we had tripled up the bow and stern lines, doubled up the spring lines, and put the right kind of knots in each line.

During lunch, our waitress had explained to us where the public marina was. So with our constant boating companions, fear and trepidation, we cast off all ten lines and motored downwind a mile or so. Then we turned into the wind and the current and entered the sanctuary of the breakwater.

Laurie was below and I was putting the wind screen up around our spray dodger when a big fish buying tender came cowboying alongside of us. The channel was very narrow; he was about 120 tons or so, 70 or more feet long, and going about five knots. He should have been going about one knot. He jammed it into reverse and tried to stop that 120 tons of stuff right alongside my small 28 foot boat. His single screw swung his high transom to port directly towards the middle of my boat. I had visions of our boat being crushed, with Laurie down below, as he somehow managed to slide his transom overhang forward over my bow. He only ripped out one stanchion.

No need to argue with him about who would pay for the damage to my boat because another Miller Law of the Sea prevailed. "The biggest boat always has the right of way." He hollered down at me,

"A lot of commercial boats'll be coming in here in the next hour or so. Get that frou frou lookin' boat out'a there!"

Another of MILLER'S LAWS OF THE SEA, "The guy who hollers first and the loudest, from the highest point, is the one who gets obeyed."

Laurie and I had exhausted our options. We had survived the 63 mph winds and waves and our only damage on the entire trip occurred while we were tied up to the dock.

We moved the boat.

"We found out later that the wind was gusting as high as 63 mph."

DINGHY DRIVERS

I live on an island during the summer; the other day I was driving my 20 foot powerboat over to the marina to buy a few parts so I could fix something that was broken. There, I got to watch, in awe, as an overweight skipper from Iowa, Colorado, Kansas, or maybe even Utah tried to maneuver his chartered 52 foot houseboat, so he could tie it up to a buoy for the night.

Buoys are cheaper to tie up to than a dock.

After a dozen or so passes on either side of the buoy and a lot of shouting between he, his guests, and anyone else within earshot to, "shut up," said skipper finally moved his floating Winnebago away from the buoy about 100 yards. I assumed he did this so he could make a good run at it. However, another sequence of shouting, screaming, and swearing in four different languages followed, as the skipper and his guests finally decided on plan "B."

"Launch the dinghy so we can row a line to the buoy and then we can haul the big boat up to it, so we can tie up for the night."

Simple enough.

Wrong.

The winch on the davit for the dinghy was a hand crank with a large, mechanical advantage set of gears and a case of near-terminal starvation for lack of grease or maintenance. The rope that was wound around the windlass was last used to lasso a horse in a John Wayne movie, 40 years ago.

Old rope seems to be a disease of el cheapo rent-a-boat companies.

The dinghy seemed to be off balance just a little bit as they got it up off its resting place on the top of the boat. With a great deal of effort, they swung it out over the water. As they did, the stern of the dinghy drooped until it was hanging at a 70 degree angle, instead of horizontal.

"No problem. It's because of the outboard motor."

The guest/deckhand who was manually operating the dinghy winch handle made the mistake of thinking that, because it was hard to turn, it had some kind of a brake on it.

Wrong again.

With a mind of its own, the weight of the dingy started to make the winch handle revolve at an increasingly rapid rate, until it was much too dangerous to try to grab it. The dinghy was starting to drop towards the water at a speed that no one wanted it to.

One of the guests was a physics teacher at a university somewhere; he grabbed a big piece of lumber that was holding some other stuff up off the deck and attempted to thrust it into the now rapidly whirling winch handle.

It spit out that two-by-four like a watermelon seed from a ten-year-old's mouth and the broken end of the two-by-four shot right through the back window of the chartered yacht.

The dinghy just kept on dropping towards the water, where it went down stern first, looking not unlike the Titanic after it hit the iceberg.

Once the dinghy was awash in the water behind the boat, there was no more tension on the winch rope, so the handle gradually came to a stop.

The saga continues.

An electric pump was lowered into the dinghy and the water pouring out of it gradually brought it up to float properly.

Time was running out, so the captain of OLD LEAKY decided that he had to make one or two more runs at the buoy because the outboard motor was now saltwater flooded and a diligent search didn't reveal where the oars for the dinghy had been stowed.

By now, half a dozen other boats had gathered in a semicircle to watch this entire intricate execution of a sporting event requiring such unusual coordination. They all stayed at least 75 yards away for safety's sake.

As the Colorado, Utah, or Kansas Captain attempted to drive his boat closer and closer to the buoy, he missed it once again. Screaming in anger, he now jammed both throttles into reverse.

Forgetting, of course, that he had a dinghy attached to the back of his yacht by a nylon rope. A nylon rope that could tow an eighteen-wheel truck. As the big boat started to back up, the nylon rope began to sink to a depth where it began to be silently and unceremoniously wound up around the port propeller.

There was so much confusion on the flying bridge at this time, that no one in command noticed a drop in the rpm of the port engine as the dinghy rope began to wind around that prop like a giant fishing reel.

As it did, the dinghy began to glide closer and closer to the transom of the bigger yacht, until there was almost no rope left and the bow of the dinghy began to point down towards the port propeller. It was then slowly sucked under water, where it was chewed up by that same propeller like a carrot in a Cuisinart.

Still, no one up on the bridge noticed anything different until the made-in-Japan outboard motor began to go two falls out of three with that same port prop. They both lost.

It cost $647 to have a scuba diver go underwater and remove the prop, untangle the nylon rope, and have a new prop flown in from Seattle to replace the slightly bent one.

The genuine Japanese outboard motor is now a small fishing reef in the vicinity of buoy #7-B.

And, by the time I got to the marine hardware store for the parts to fix my boat, it was closed.

"They had an El-cheapo-rent-a-boat that looked like a floating Winnebago."

THE ARROW

Where Ernest came from, no one really knew. He was on the ski patrol when I was living in the parking lot in Sun Valley in 1947. Ernest stood about 5' 10", was very husky, extremely good looking, with a thick head of straight, coal black hair, a dark complexion, and he was very, very quiet. He moved with the calculated, simple grace of a mountain lion, and, at parties, he never drank or womanized. There were all kinds of rumors about his background and when you were talking to him and looked into his dark brown, almost black, piercing eyes, you knew there was always something very powerful lurking behind them. There was no way you could read them. I don't think anyone knew for sure what his real background was, but the often-told story of his life unfolded like this:

He was rumored to be a half-breed Native American Indian, with a full-blooded Sioux father and a mother who was French Canadian. He had served well in World War II as a scout in the famed Tenth Mountain Division Ski troops. When people talked about him in almost reverent whispers, various numbers were used about his extraordinary war exploits. They ranged from half a dozen incidents, to an impossible 100 or so.

He took no rifle with him to fight the war in Europe. He was so uncanny with a bow and arrow that it was whispered that he had learned his skills from his father, who learned them from his grandfather, Chief Flying Hawk, nephew of Sitting Bull and brother of Kicking Bear.

It was said,

"With his bow and arrow, Ernest could shoot and kill small game from the back of a galloping horse."

Some even said,

"Ernest could hit a bird in flight."

It was believed by everyone, who repeated it and expanded a little on the story, that they had heard from someone else, that,

"Ernest had stolen behind enemy lines and killed more than a dozen enemy soldiers with his very silent bow and arrows."

Sometimes, in the employee cafeteria when he was sitting off in a corner by himself nurturing a cup of black coffee, it was easy to imagine him at war, silently stealing through the trees and across the newfallen snow. At exactly the right moment in the black of night with the almost noiseless twang of his bowstring, an unsuspecting sentry would topple over dead, one of Ernest's silent arrows sticking out of his chest just below the left collarbone and right through his heart.

Then, just as silently, he would begin to map the perimeter defenses of the enemy lines, sneaking back across the lines before dawn and reporting to his sergeant,

"It's all clear in that sector for the morning assault."

Only once did I ever see the results of Ernest's bow and arrow skills.

The ducks and geese that wintered at the head of Dollar Lake, near the bridge that ran over Trail Creek, were almost too fat to fly. They spent the winter living on great handouts of leftover food from the Lodge dining room. On occasions, however, a stray dog or some guest would scare them up into flight and they would laboriously circle the Challenger Inn a few times, all the while honking very loudly.

More than once during the winter, my roommate in the parking lot, Ward and I, were awakened by the loud honking of those fat geese as they flew low over our small trailer in the parking lot. It took the geese about three or four laps around the village to gain very much altitude. Then, as though it was way too much work to fly any longer, they would splash back down in the same, small, unfrozen place where Trail Creek flowed into Dollar lake and wait for their next handout.

In the grey dawn of one below zero morning, we were awakened by all six of the Trail Creek geese in flight. One of them, however, sounded very different. His honking was high pitched and sounded very labored, almost wheezing. I didn't think too much about it, except that I had never heard them fly this early before. I did know, however, that no one would go down to the river that early in the morning just to scare the geese and ducks so they could watch them fly around the village.

The second time the flock flew honking over our camp ground, I stuck my head out of the trailer door in time to catch a glimpse of them. Something was definitely wrong with one of them. He had another goose flying unusually close to him and his neck was at a very weird angle for the normal, graceful flight of a goose. Hoping they would circle once again, I got out of bed for a better look.

I didn't get out of my mummy sleeping bag; I just stood up in it outside the trailer and watched for them when they came into view the next time they came over the parking lot. They hadn't gained any more altitude, whatsoever.

The goose with the peculiar sound and the strange bend in his neck had an arrow sticking right through it. His beautiful white breast was covered with blood, and it was very obvious that he was going to eventually crash somewhere soon.

It was later said that,

"Ernest had already poached two deer and an elk with his powerful bow and arrow and had decided that a goose or two might add some variety to the annual ski patrol big game dinner."

In the ski patrol dormitory, about the same time the wounded goose crash-landed in front of the Opera House, Ernest was silently packing his clothes, his skis, his bow, and his quiver with one arrow missing. He wasn't at the ski patrol party that night, but was last seen walking south out of Ketchum with a substantial load on his shoulders.

"It was obvious that he was going to crash land somewhere soon."

HOW TO MOVE
TO SNOW COUNTRY

You have already made the decision to move to a ski resort. No more driving on ice all night Friday night and skidding through freezing rain Sunday drives back home. No more kids throwing up in the back seat because you got tired of franchised food and decided to try a truck stop. No more staggering towards your rented condo, only to find nine Athabasca Ski Club members stretched out on the floor for the night.

What do you take with you on this change of lifestyle move?

Keep a couple of things in mind as you wander through the house you are trying to sell. As you list it for sale, your home has become your "4 bdr. 3 bth. 2 car grg. landscp. cls. to strs. schs. grt. interior, two firplc., will finance," house. (Do you really think you can get three times what you paid for it?)

Anything that you haven't used in six months, put in the garage and sell for any amount anyone will give you for it. Or better still, give it away. That darling cocktail dress or those saddle shoes won't be needed when it's ten below zero and the furnace isn't working.

Anything the kids currently own will be instantly obsolete in the mountains. The rad $200 skateboard won't work on the dirt road that leads to your, someday-to-be-paved, driveway. Nintendo will be replaced with push-ups by your kids, because of a local Norwegian ski coach you will get to know. You will have to get a second or third job so you can support him or her.

Any budget you have for ski equipment must automatically be increased by a factor of at least four: your kids need giant slalom skis, downhill skis, slalom skis, packed snow skis, and powder skis; they will also need a snowboard and a 'rad', salvation army outfit when riding it. And your wife can't be seen in the same outfit more than once a week.

Do you bring your gardening tools?

What for?

The deer will eat the fruit trees you plant and the rabbits will fight the deer for the flowers.

If you have a dog, bring a couple of cases of tomato juice. Abby, your golden retriever, will somehow find every skunk within three miles and the local vet charges $100 for a skunk deodorant bath.

Computers? Bring yours along so you can use it to try to balance your rapidly diminishing working capital, as the septic tank freezes and, after thawing, runs over into the well, then freezes again. It's always at least eleven below zero when you have finally figured out what the problem is.

Buy a chain saw and try to cut down your own trees for your firewood. This can save you a lot of money unless you have never chopped down a tree before. If that is the case, you will probably cut one down near a back road somewhere and drop it right down the middle of the windshield of the new Minivan that you just paid $28,795 for. The concussion will explode the air bag and you can't get behind the steering wheel to drive home unless you cut a hole in the air bag.

Work clothes? Bring a lot of them because you will need a lot of them. Scuff them up a bit with sandpaper so you don't go into the local hardware store looking like you just moved here from the city.

Do you buy all of your hardware or supplies locally or bring them up from the city? Do both, because the local hardware store will be one of two kinds. If you're lucky, they will have every nut and bolt that has been made since 1734, if they can just find it. The owner will be able to tell you how to fix anything, even though you can't do it when you follow his directions. His wife will have blue hair and be wearing a baggy, flowered, cotton dress over her corset, Ben Franklin glasses on a chain around her neck, and nurse's shoes.

Or worse yet, the alternate local hardware store will be run by someone who moved here from the city and bought the old one. He and his new wife, his second marriage, her first, decided to make it into a designer hardware store. They carry only spare parts for Italian faucets and German stoves, French gardening tools, and seeds and feed imported from South America. They also carry stainless steel shovels and carts to sit on when you are weeding, or designer wheelbarrows and solar powered compost bins. They have 19 books on how to make a patio for less than $10,000 and three different editions of "Hot Tubs for Fun and Profit." A lot of ferns are hanging in the windows and their new age music sounds like a flock of seagulls trying to grab the last fish out of the live bait tank.

You used to be able to buy a *Sears Catalog* and shop by the light of your Coleman lantern. Speaking of that, you'd better have some spare mantels and an extra can of white gas because the electricity goes out at least once a week in Chalet Country.

For that day of days, YOUR MOVING DAY, you will need a U-Haul trailer and a moving van company. At $200 an hour for The Starving Students Moving and Storage Company, make sure you have what's left of your city possessions in cardboard boxes when they arrive. Otherwise, you will blow your first nine months' mortgage payments just getting to that "Little Chalet In The Sky."

Will your new four-on-the-floor convertible work in the snow? Of course it will, but the heater in it won't. Buy a new fur coat for your wife so she can drive it. It's a tossup whether the new coat or a new car will be the best investment. If you opt for a fur coat, make sure that you have all of the certificates of suicide for all of the pelts in the coat, because there are bound to be animal activists in the community. An animal activist is usually someone whose husband isn't a good enough hunter to trap the animals for her coat or can't afford to buy her one.

Easing into the community can take as long as a decade or as short as two decades.

By then, your wife will be on the ski patrol, your daughter will be tending bar when she comes home from Vassar for Christmas vacation, and you will still be trying to make the furnace work whenever it gets below 45 degrees fahrenheit in your living room.

This is assuming you have already chosen your perfect hideaway in the hills. You chose it so you could go skiing every day. Except when it is cloudy, very cold, a little icy, you have to go to town for groceries, or the furnace doesn't work and you have to stand by for three weeks waiting for the handyman to keep his appointment with you.

If you are dumb enough to try to build your own place in paradise, you have a lot to learn. There are more seasons in ski country than you can ever imagine, seasons when workers don't show up, powder snow season, deer season, trout season, elk season, mud season, and divorce season.

The contractor you choose will be someone who drives a pickup truck with a rack in the back window. Depending on the time of the year, the rack will have either a rifle, fishing pole, shotgun, or baseball bat hanging in it. A broom will be standing up in the corner of the truck bed by the cab and a black labrador retriever will be barking in the back. He will have a red bandana around his neck and the driver of the truck will be talking through his beard on his cellular phone. You think he is ordering supplies for your new house: he is talking to the bank loan officer and trying to get an advance on the draw to dig your foundation. He needs that money so he can pay the bills for the house he is supposed to have just finished, but went too far over budget and couldn't.

He will talk to you about frost heaves, maybes, self-curing cement, natural stone, cubic feet per minute, and a lot of other stuff that you can pretend to understand. What he is doing is sizing you up so he can figure out how steep he can stiff you when he starts to build your dream Chalet.

You could buy an existing house of headaches instead.

But, don't believe the previous owner or the real estate agent. Their job is to move property. Your job is to try to rent the place for a year, instead of buying it. That way you can find out if, in fact, you can move here full-time and live on twice as much as you ever earned in the city. Or, is the myth of ski resort living just that, a myth?

Do you really want to live in that Chalet beside the slope so you can ski in and ski out? If so, all of your freeloading friends can now park their cars for free in your driveway, blocking your garage, and stop by after skiing every day to have tea. This will lead to the use of your bathrooms, showers and jacuzzi, and calling out for pizza. You get to pay for the pizzas because they will have spent all of their money for lunch at the top of the mountain and the pizza deliveryman won't take Visa Cards. They naively thought they could buy a hamburger and a cup of coffee for two for under 20 dollars. They shared a hot dog and a can of Coke for the same 20 bucks. The resort insists it is priced that way because the freight to haul it to the top of the mountain is so much.

What about wardrobe selection for moving to the Chalet in the sky?

Beware of invitations that say black tie optional. You will be the only guy there in a tweed suit. All of the women will be dressed like they are going to the inaugural of the President of the United States.

Most resorts require the use of every glitzy garment that you could ever buy or use in the city. They call it Mountain Elegance. That is mountain talk for very expensive, slinky, and has to be worn under a new fur coat of some kind.

Then, there is the outdoor wardrobe. You thought you could get away with only ski clothes. You need a pair of Sorrells for when you use the rotary snowplow to clean out your driveway. Oh yes! The rotary snowplows that do the job start at about $1,000. Make sure the Sorrels look used. They will if you drag them behind your car on the first four or five trips you make to the supermarket.

The supermarket is usually half the size of your local convenience store, nine miles away, and only charges 27.5% more.

Get used to catalog buying. And get used to catalog saving. Once you make your first purchase, your name moves through the catalog company lists like an avalanche in the Caribous. Have a place to store those catalogs, preferably by the fireplace because you will get a lot of them and this will save on log burning. In one two week period while we were away, my wife received 44 pounds of them. She had purchased a 19 dollar sugar bowl as a wedding present for the son of a friend in Canada and in those two weeks, we got enough catalogs to use up most of a 70-year-old pine tree.

Furniture for your move?

Be sure to buy a lot of mattresses. You will have a lot of freeloading company. Make sure the mattresses are very uncomfortable. Air mattresses are best because, when you turn down the furnace during the night, the air contracts. If you inflate them just right, the mattress will sag until at least 29% of the guest's body rests on the floor. The mattress is just soft enough not to have to climb out of bed and blow it back up. But, the floor is hard enough so your guests wake up exhausted. If they stay the third night, you have failed Air Mattress Inflation, 1-A.

Would I move to Snow Country again? I did, and yes, I would again.

I haven't seen a drive-by shooting since I have lived here, except for the poachers who nailed a deer in my front yard last October. I haven't been mugged yet, if you dismiss the mugging I get every morning when I buy my ski lift ticket. There are no pockets of poverty here, except the neighborhood where I live, and when it isn't snowing hard, I can see blue sky instead of smog. They are, however, trying to pass an ordinance so you can't burn anything in your fireplace, except during July and August. Other than that, moving to Snow Country is a great, expensive idea.

"The contractor you choose will drive a pickup truck with a rack in the back window."

THE GOOD OLD DAYS

As the quad chairlift cleared the loading ramp and accelerated to 2,800 feet a minute, we lowered the foot rest and the fellow sitting next to me said,

"Look at all them snowboards down there! And did ya see all them expensive ski clothes on those rich folks in the lift line? Skiing sure wasn't like this in the good old days!"

He spoke with a lot of experience, if you judged him by his ski gear. He wore a pair of tight, faded navy blue, bell bottom stretch pants with the seam sewed down the front, a pair of leather Hadderer boots, a faded navy blue and Chinese red Sportcaster hip length quilted parka, and K-2 Hamburger skis with Cubco bindings. This guy had been making the ski scene since before there was a ski scene.

His comment,

"Sure wasn't like this in the good old days!" started me thinking.

Just how good were the good old days?

The good thing was, you could ride a chairlift all day for $4, but most ski resorts only had one lift. It carried about 400 skiers an hour, one person at a time, and on most weekends, the lift line was always over a half hour long. Ski resort wages were almost fifty cents an hour. (I managed to earn about $100 a month in those days.)

"Been skiing forty-three years now, and never took a lesson. Why start now?"

Most of the things we take for granted today had not been invented when Ward Baker and I spent the winter of 1946-47 living in the Sun Valley, Idaho, parking lot. The good thing about living there for three and a half months in an eight foot long trailer? We skied every day for eighteen cents a day.

But, I get ahead of myself.

When we snuck on the chairlifts every day, we had a few handicaps by today's standards of skiing.

For example, here are just a few of the things that no one had invented yet:

Safety bindings (or release bindings as they are called today)? When you fell, your skis stayed on and your leg sometimes fell off. Or, at least it just revolved, independent of your body. For a lot of money, a doctor would tell you,

"You have a spiral."

Plastic ski boots? Instead, we wore soft, leather boots that reached all the way up to our ankle bone. Today, they wouldn't even be considered support enough for cross country skiing.

Thermal long underwear? When our wool long johns got wet, they made us itch so badly we could barely sit in a chairlift while we rode back up.

Waterproof clothes? Forget it. No such thing as a nylon parka existed then, much less a quilted parka. One day, White Stag hired me to ski in a half poplin and half Nylon Parka to see which arm stayed the warmest; they were on the cutting edge of ski industry testing!

Metal and fiberglass skis that turned easily? Forget that too. Everyone skied on stiff hickory boards that were so long they reached to your outstretched hand held high over your head. Unless your skis were 7' 6" long, you were considered a whimp.

Grooming machinery? Nope! Racers side-stepped down a slalom or a downhill course to pack it the day before the race. Otherwise, forget it.

Snow tires? No such thing. Skid chains cost $4.95 a pair and took an hour and a half to put on. You did this while you wallowed around in the mud, just below the altitude where the rain turned to snow.

Quad chairlifts? They didn't even have double chairlifts until 1949. You rode all alone in wind and snow and rain. There was no way to cozy up to that ski companion of your dreams. When the lift broke, which it often did, you hoped you were close enough to the ground to take off your skis and jump. Otherwise, you just sat there and froze until they somehow got the lift running again before nightfall.

Where to go skiing? In 1946, they hadn't yet invented Squaw Valley, Heavenly Valley, Blackcomb, Whistler, Vail, Sugarbush, Snowbird, Crystal Mountain, Boyne Mountain, Stratton, Mt. Snow, or Killington, to mention just a few. But a pioneer here and there was buying a couple of thousand feet of Navy Surplus manila hemp rope, an old car, nailed a few sheaves to some trees, built a rope tow, and called it a ski resort. A rope tow, an outhouse, and a muddy parking lot were the only amenities available. You ate your peanut butter sandwich lunch in your car and if you knew someone who was rich, they might rent a Motel for $5 a night. After going to the twenty-five cent movie in town, they might sneak your carload of friends and their sleeping bags into their unit and let them sleep on the floor for fifty cents a body.

Rent a condo? Not invented yet.

Sun Valley, Idaho, slept 846 people in 1946. If you were good with tools, you remodeled the back seat of your car so you could sleep in it in the muddy rope tow parking lot and cook your meals over a Coleman stove. A few years later, Ed's Bed's would come on the scene in Aspen at $3 a night.

Interstate Highways? A ski resort is in the mountains. Right? Who wants to go to those places, especially in the winter? No one. Why should the taxpayers widen a road over a pass or build a tunnel under a pass to get to a rope tow or a couple of T bars? Forget it. From Denver to Aspen was a seven or eight hour drive on a snow and ice-covered, two lane road, up over 13,000 foot Loveland Pass and then 11,000 foot Vail Pass, and the road was two lanes wide all the way with eighteen wheelers crawling up over both passes at five or six miles an hour.

Check your skis on your flight? No way! In 1952, the first few times I flew to film a ski resort, they had to slide my skis under the three back seats of a tail-dragging DC-3. Los Angeles to Europe involved staying overnight in New York after a ten hour first leg of the trip. Then New York to Newfoundland to Scotland, with the navigator of the DC-4 taking occasional star sights with a sextant to rediscover where we were in relation to where we were supposed to be.

The good old days were:

Driving without snow tires, power brakes, power steering, automatic transmission, or four wheel drive. This was only slightly compensated for because gasoline cost twenty cents a gallon.

Standing in a 45 minute lift line with itchy, wet, long underwear because my $7 gaberdine ski pants weren't waterproof; feeling the water seeping in through the holes in my lace up boots; trying to keep my goggles from fogging up while watching the ski patrol haul yet another broken-legged body off the hill because of wearing bear trap bindings, was really "The Good Old Days."

Give me skiing today on a run that was groomed last night, before a foot or so of new powder fell. Let me ride up in a high speed Quad lift with a Plexiglass cover while bundled up in a layered ski suit, wearing plastic boots with heaters, warm gloves, thermal underwear, a pair of fog-proof goggles, tuned just right safety bindings, lightweight poles, and a pair of the new, soft, fat skis to carve up yet another untracked, powder snow, ski slope.

I started making turns on a pair of $2 Spaulding pine skis with toe straps in 1937. Since then, fortunately, the inventors of ski stuff have kept ahead of my ability to need the latest and the greatest invention for my falling-behind physical condition. I appreciate them for all of this research and development because the warranties on my deteriorating body have already run out. Each "Good Old Day" is getting better than the last one!

271